As one of the world's longest establis[hed]
and best-known travel bran[ds]
Thomas Cook are the experts in tra[vel]

For more than 135 years [our]
guidebooks have unlocked the secr[ets]
of destinations around the wo[rld]
sharing with travellers a wealth of
experience and a passion for travel.

**Rely on Thomas Cook as your
travelling companion on your next trip
and benefit from our unique heritage.**

Thomas Cook **traveller** guides

PUGLIA
Zoë Ross

Your travelling companion since 1873

Written and updated by Zoë Ross
Original photography by Robin Gauldie

Published by Thomas Cook Publishing
A division of Thomas Cook Tour Operations Limited
Company registration no. 3772199 England
The Thomas Cook Business Park, Unit 9, Coningsby Road,
Peterborough PE3 8SB, United Kingdom
E-mail: books@thomascook.com, Tel: + 44 (0) 1733 416477
www.thomascookpublishing.com

Produced by Cambridge Publishing Management Limited
Burr Elm Court, Main Street, Caldecote CB23 7NU
www.cambridgepm.co.uk

ISBN: 978-1-84848-368-2

© 2007, 2009 Thomas Cook Publishing
This third edition © 2011
Text © Thomas Cook Publishing
Maps © Thomas Cook Publishing/PCGraphics (UK) Limited

Series Editor: Karen Beaulah
Production/DTP: Steven Collins

Printed and bound in Spain by GraphyCems

Cover photography © Spila Riccardo/SIME-4Corners Images

All rights reserved. No part of this publication may be reproduced, stored in
a retrieval system or transmitted, in any form or by any means, electronic,
mechanical, recording or otherwise, in any part of the world, without prior
permission of the publisher. Requests for permission should be made to the
publisher at the above address.

Although every care has been taken in compiling this publication, and the
contents are believed to be correct at the time of printing, Thomas Cook Tour
Operations Limited cannot accept any responsibility for errors or omissions,
however caused, or for changes in details given in the guidebook, or for the
consequences of any reliance on the information provided. Descriptions and
assessments are based on the author's views and experiences when writing and
do not necessarily represent those of Thomas Cook Tour Operations Limited.

Contents

Introduction

If Italy is commonly referred to as the 'boot' because of its geographical shape, then Puglia (or Apulia in the English translation) is its 'heel'. This largely flat landscape of rolling countryside, very much dependent on its agricultural successes, has remarkably so far escaped the mass tourism that has long been a blight or boon to the rest of the country. Gradually, however, more curious travellers, seeking to escape the crowds of Tuscany or Umbria, are beginning to move south and discover its delights.

The area is also referred to as the *mezzogiorno* – the 'midday' – and this nickname is apt for its allusion to the slow pace of life and sleepy ambience of the noonday sun. Within a day of being in the region, it becomes apparent that Italians in this part of the world very much work to live, rather than the other way around. Little will get in the way of their traditional and unshakeable siesta, when entire towns and villages batten down the hatches and shut up shop for as much as five hours, leaving bemused visitors strolling through ghostly streets and echoing alleyways, bereft of any human activity.

And bemusement works both ways. Tourism has never been the mainstay of the economy here, and this is one of the few remaining corners of Europe where a visitor can be made to feel an object of fascination, if not intrusion, by locals nonplussed by a foreign face. That's not to say the locals are at all

Basilica di Santa Croce, Lecce

unwelcoming, but there's certainly no sense of the fawning attitude that accompanies experiences in places more reliant on vacation wallets.

At the heart of Puglian life is tradition, in all senses. The prevalence of Catholicism in the region means that the tiniest village will boast an often incongruously impressive church, or even cathedral. And while most of the towns' outskirts are an unattractive hotchpotch of post-war apartment buildings and commercial properties, at their heart are lovingly preserved historic centres that are almost living museums in themselves, dating back hundreds of years. And if the siesta is a stubbornly immovable custom, so too is the *passeggiata*, the evening stroll through the streets as the towns reawaken and people come together for coffee, an ice cream and a gossip.

Puglia is not a destination for visitors in search of sun and sand. While the heat in summer can be relentless and parts of the coastline do strive to appeal to this sort of holiday, the natural landscape remains reluctant and, in comparison to the Mediterranean, the facilities are at best half-hearted. It is, however, a wonderful coastline for scrambling around rock pools and feasting on the sea's bounty in simple but accomplished seafood *trattorie* (restaurants). It's a region too that is a treasure trove for history buffs, whether it be the archaeological sites and museums that recall days of Greek and Roman inhabitants, medieval castles and fortresses aplenty, or the breathtaking artistry of 18th-century Baroque architecture in towns such as Lecce and Martina Franca. Above all, though, Puglia offers a chance to immerse yourself in an Italy staunchly lived the Italian way, in all its interpretations – proud, traditional, family-oriented and with people of the soil. As a visitor you are welcome, but no time-honoured routine is going to be disrupted by tourist vagaries; for the holidaymaker, the phrase 'come to heel' has never been more apt.

Introduction

Dramatic coastline at Vieste

The land

The small region of Puglia in the 'heel' of Italy's 'boot' is often referred to as the 'land of the two seas', occupying a space between the Adriatic and the Ionian. It's a predominantly flat region, with only the mountain forest of the Gargano Peninsula offering any kind of significant height above sea level, although the hilltop towns around the Valle d'Itria and the ravines of the rupestrian *(rocky) villages in Taranto region give the impression of vertiginous slopes.*

The region is divided into six provinces – Foggia, Barletta-Andria-Trani, Bari, Brindisi, Lecce (and Salento) and Taranto – with the capital of the entire region based in the city of Bari. Most of the region is given over to agriculture, although there are industrial sites in the regions of Foggia and Taranto, and the increasing presence of wind farms.

One of Puglia's many olive groves

The vegetation is relatively uniform, with the landscape dotted with pine trees, almond trees, prickly pears and, along the coast, palms. And, of course, there is kilometre upon kilometre of beautiful olive groves and vineyards, which clearly illustrate why this region of Italy produces the most olive oil and wine. Aside from olives and grapes, the other main product here is wheat, as seen in the rolling fields that define the *tavoliere* plain (literally 'tableland') in the Foggia district. This varies slightly once you move south of Lecce, where the olives give way in part to *macchia* (scrubland) and wild herbs and rocket (*arugula*) grow in abundance along the roadsides. Sheep and cattle are the main breeding stock for farmers.

Intriguingly, this is an area of microclimates, which has helped to make the wines produced here of superior quality. A short journey of 20 minutes or so from one town to another can lead to a significant change in temperature and atmosphere.

The land

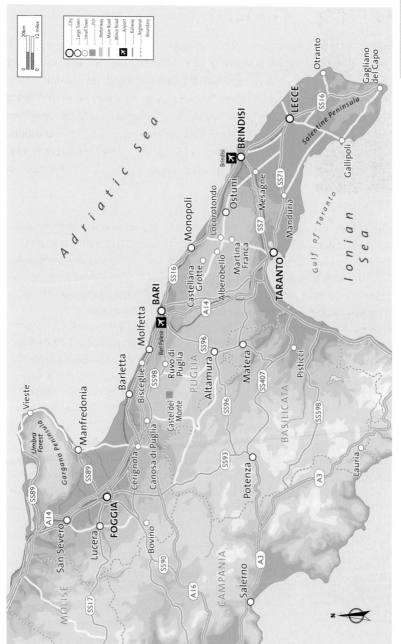

History

c.50,000 BC Evidence has been discovered of Neanderthal remains, proving that this region was occupied in Palaeolithic times.

1700 BC Mycenaeans and Minoans occupy the land.

c.760 BC Greek settlers found Taranto, Otranto and other towns in the region, then known as Magna Graecia, and trade with the north.

275 BC The Romans defeat the Greeks at Beneventum and occupy the whole of Italy.

216 BC As part of the Punic Wars, Hannibal and his Carthaginian troops invade Cannae, beating the Romans and massacring most of the town.

190 BC The great Roman Road, the Via Appia, extends to Brindisi.

19 BC The great Roman poet Virgil dies in Brindisi.

AD 535 The Roman Empire splits in two and southern Italy is controlled by the eastern Empire, Byzantium.

847 Bari becomes the provincial capital under the Saracens.

1056 The Normans begin their successful attempt to oust the Byzantines from the region and establish a kingdom in Sicily.

1071 Bari is captured by Robert Guiscard.

1087 The remains of St Nicholas (San Nicola) are stolen from Turkey and brought to Bari.

1220 Frederick II, Holy Roman Emperor, begins his 30-year domination of the area, building defensive castles throughout Puglia.

1241 Frederick II is excommunicated by Pope Innocent IV because of his constant battles for power against the Papacy.

1250 Frederick II dies near Lucera.

1254 Manfred, son of Frederick II, becomes King of Sicily and controls most of the southern region.

1266	Charles of Anjou wrests control from Manfred.
1435	The Spaniard Alfonso of Aragon takes control of the region. Spain rules for 200 years until the War of Spanish Succession.
1480	Turkish invaders attack Otranto, making martyrs out of 800 citizens who refuse to renounce their Christian faith.
1503	The French invade Puglia at Barletta but are defeated.
1627	The Gargano Peninsula is struck by an earthquake.
1660–1710	Giuseppe Zimbalo leads the Baroque explosion of architecture in Lecce.
1731	An earthquake strikes the region around Foggia.
1860–61	Vittorio Emanuele II, King of Sardinia, conquers the south. Puglia is divided into three provinces: Foggia, Bari and Lecce.
1870	*Risorgimento*, the Unification of Italy.
1918	Padre Pio experiences his first stigmata (*see p29*).
1925	Benito Mussolini launches the 'Battle of Wheat' to try to make the country self-sufficient.
1938	The grottoes of Castellana (*see p62*) are discovered.
1940	The British attack the Italian Navy at Taranto in a surprise air strike during World War II.
1946–7	Post-war inflation and the poverty of the south lead to violent clashes between farm workers and police.
1948	The Republic of Italy is declared.
1991	The skeleton of Delia, the Neolithic pregnant woman, is found near Ostuni (*see p76*).
2002	Italy adopts the euro.
2009	The new province of Barletta-Andria-Trani is created.
2010	The body of Padre Pio, exhumed in 2008, is put on display in San Giovanni Rotondo (*see p39*). Some believe this will become a greater pilgrimage site than Lourdes.

Megaliths and menhirs

The evidence of Messapian inhabitants in Puglia some time around the Bronze Age period (1700 BC and onwards) has been proved by various archaeological excavations that have revealed and dated the ancient megaliths and menhirs in the region. One of the main areas of settlement was in modern-day Salento, and many menhirs can be seen in the countryside and along roadsides around the cities of Lecce and Taranto, and particularly around the Urugano villages of Martano and Corigliano d'Otranto (see p95).

Megaliths are a collection of large stones grouped together, presumably heaved by an army of strong-armed people – no one has been able to explain their construction. Their meaning, too, remains mysterious and unknown, but many historians have formed the conclusion that megaliths were used as some kind of astronomical guide, indicating that settlers were aware of the importance of the universe on their daily lives (the world's most famous megalith is Stonehenge in the UK). If true, it is proof that scientific knowledge was in play long before the arrival of the Romans. Menhirs, in contrast, are long, tall single stones, averaging about 5m (16½ft) in height, that were thought to mark burial plots or to honour deceased leaders, much in the same way that statues are erected to commemorate great men or women in the modern world. Dolmens can also be found in Puglia. Similar to megaliths, dolmens included a stone 'lid', which is often covered with mounds (specchie), and they were used as burial tombs.

One of the most important surviving Messapian areas is Manduria (see p107), where ancient walls and a series of megaliths have survived the centuries. At Rocca Vecchia (literally 'old rock'), on the coast east of Lecce, there are remains of megalithic walls, menhirs and caves. One of the region's most evocative dolmens stands at Montalbano, near Ostuni – alone amid swathes of olive groves, it is an eerie and rather romantic image of a past long gone. Bisceglie, too, has an important dolmen just outside town known as La Chianca (see p55). Excavations at sites such as these have uncovered a whole host of ancient artefacts, including pieces of ceramics, vases and bronze

Dolmen near Cisternino

items, and these have revealed far more about the ancient inhabitants than had previously been known. Most of these items have now been added to the collections of museums in Lecce, Taranto and Gallipoli.

The isolated and, in many cases, rather neglected state of these ancient monuments may seem surprising in a country that is otherwise so careful to preserve its long and fascinating history. However, excavations are ongoing, and more and more are beginning to be protected by way of fences and restricted public access.

Politics

A former hotchpotch of individual kingdoms and dynasties, not to mention a land strongly influenced by the Papacy, Italy finally became a united kingdom in 1870 after the long campaign of the Risorgimento. *In 1948, after the horrors of World War II and the Fascist government of Mussolini, Italy became a republic, ruled by the elected president and prime minister rather than a monarch. There are 20 defined regions in Italy, of which Puglia occupies the entire 'heel' of the country's 'boot'.*

Italy, and the south in particular, has long had a reputation of political corruption, and worse, although this was somewhat alleviated by changes made after the *mani pullite* (dirty hands) investigations in the 1980s which brought underhand political dealings to public attention. Since 1994 the country has been largely dominated by the centre-right politics of the controversial Silvio Berlusconi, who has held the position of prime minister

Taranto's regional government building

three times. He was most recently re-elected in 2008, following the surprise downfall of the opposition led by Romano Prodi. His determined hold over the Italian people is in evidence in areas such as his ownership of various TV channels, thereby controlling much of the nation's viewing. Moreover, there remain in the Italian mentality perhaps the strongest Communist leanings in all of western Europe. Indeed, since 2005, the president of Puglia has been the Communist (and, controversially for a Catholic country, openly homosexual) leader Nichi Vendola, who managed to retain his position in January 2010 despite repeated challenges from more right-wing parties. Regional presidents are elected for a five-year term. However, the Communists are unlikely ever to be elected into national power.

Puglia's economy is governed by agriculture. Consequently, the pressures that associations such as Confagricola are able to put on governments in order to improve their lot are vitally important. Puglia is the richest region of the traditionally poor south because of its high output of agricultural products. Over the past couple of decades industry has also added to the economy, particularly in the areas of steel production and the manufacturing of textiles.

The Palazzo del Governo in Bari

Culture

True culture vultures may be disappointed in Puglia. Unlike the great northern Italian provinces, this area in the south is sparsely served by cultural institutions apart from in Lecce, which boasts a year-round programme of theatrical, dance and music offerings. This is a region to be admired from the outside – marvelling at the architecture and absorbing the country air – rather than from the inside, soaking up highbrow entertainments.

Theatre and cinema

Lecce is the city of choice if you want to enjoy theatrical events as well as ballet, opera and classical music. Bari also enjoys a programme of events, although this is slightly less dynamic than Lecce's. The best way to find out what's on during your stay is to visit the tourist office, although you'll see posters for current happenings pinned to lampposts and tree trunks in towns and villages alike.

The main theatre in Bari is the Petruzzelli, particularly renowned for its opera productions. In Brindisi, locals have recently benefited from the Verdi Theatre, opened in 2002, with superb acoustics for its classical concerts. Almost all entertainment is presented solely in Italian, including British and American films that will have been dubbed into the native language.

Every April, Lecce hosts the Festival del Cinema Europeo (Festival of European Cinema) with offerings from all over the continent. As well as screening the latest European releases, there are retrospectives and 'themed' showings, plus an awards ceremony honouring the year's best outputs (*www.festivaldelcinemaeuropeo.it*).

Festival for Saint Oronzo, Lecce

Intricate carvings on a façade in Lecce

Architecture

Without question, one of the main highlights of a trip to Puglia is the stunning Baroque architecture that adorns the façades of Lecce and, to a lesser degree, Martina Franca (*see pp108–10*), Locorotondo (*see p63*) and Ostuni (*see pp74–6*). You can gaze for hours at the intricacies of buildings such as the Basilica di Santa Croce (*see pp84–5*) and still remain in disbelief that such art could be crafted at the hands of just a few talented men.

The architectural attractions at the other end of the artistic spectrum are the *trulli* that abound around the Valle d'Itria and are found collectively in the town of Alberobello (*see pp62–3*). These simple, round peasant 'huts' are now lovingly preserved by the Italians as both cultural gems and as tourist accommodation.

Music

Apart from the Tarantella (*see opposite*), the other significant musical offering in Puglia is its brass band tradition. Very much a music of the people, this originated when musicians travelled the countryside to entertain farmers and peasants who did not benefit from the more sophisticated operatic offerings in the towns. Today, the best-known band in this genre is the Banda Città Ruvo di Puglia, which remains perennially popular.

Various composers who hailed from Puglia and made their name in the world of 19th-century music and opera are honoured in the region – Umberto Giordano in Foggia, Giovanni Paisiello in Taranto, and Niccolò Piccinni in Bari.

Folklore

As shown by the numerous festivals that take place throughout the year in Puglia (*see pp18–19*), the area is steeped in folkloric traditions, whether recalling and 'reinventing' events from the past, or leaning towards ancient superstitions and rituals. Among the highlights are the Tarantella, the *palio* (jousting

A traditional painted cart at the Massafra museum

Children dancing at the Alberobello Festival

horse race) at Oria (*see p79*) and the Valle d'Itria Festival in summer, as well as the carnivals that precede Lent and the more sombre parades that mark Holy Week at Easter. During the summer, almost every town in the region has its own festival of some sort or another, while in autumn the grape harvest is cause for celebration.

One of the most famous folk dance troupes in the region, the Gruppo Folkloristico Città dei Trulli, is located in Alberobello and has earned itself an international reputation for its skill and energy. In August, the troupe's performance marks the finale of a festival that invites other folk groups to this small town from all over the world.

THE TARANTELLA

Italy's national folk dance, the Tarantella, is thought to have developed during a wave of panic in the 15th to 17th centuries in and around the town of Taranto. Local peasant women were supposedly bitten by tarantula spiders and infected with tarantism, believed to be venom that could only leave the body by sweating. Therefore, in part active exercise and in part hysteria, locals would dance frenetically, in pairs, in whirling circles, accompanied by quick-beat music on a mandolin. There is, however, no evidence that these spider bites were venomous, or, in fact, that the bites ever took place. Nevertheless, this tale has descended into folklore and the dance is still performed at Puglian festive occasions. The best time for the visitor to see the dance is during the San Pietro e Paolo festival in Galatina in June and July.

Festivals and events

Italy loves a good festival, and Puglia is no exception. Religion is at the core of its major events, with Easter and Christmas monopolising life at their respective times of year. But tradition and history, too, play a major part – medieval horse jousting is a wonderfully evocative re-enactment of past celebrations. And in a region that relies so heavily on its agricultural prowess there are numerous festivals that celebrate harvest time and local produce.

January

6th – to celebrate Epiphany, a horse race is held between volunteers dressed as the Magi (Mesagne)

11th – bonfires are lit in the streets and local delicacies are served (Grotte di Castellana)

February

This is carnival month, before the onset of fasting during Lent. The most important carnivals in the region are held in Putignano, Massafra and Manfredonia.

14th – a procession carrying an effigy of St Valentine draped in oranges is led through the streets (Vico del Gargano)

March

Holy Week – the week running up to Easter is celebrated throughout the region, as it is throughout the country, but the most significant and evocative celebrations are found in Taranto and Francavilla Fontana, where barefooted men (*perdoni*) dressed in hooded capes and carrying crosses walk solemnly through the town arch

April

23rd–24th – a beachside *palio* is one of the more unusual events in the Puglian calendar (Vieste)

May

2nd–11th – Barletta music concerts

7th–9th – Festa di San Nicola. This is one of Puglia's most important festivals during which a statue of St Nicholas is carried from his basilica (*see p45*) to the port, and is blessed by the bishop before being set sail on the water accompanied by a blaze of fireworks (Bari)

25th – a celebration of the cherry harvest (Leveranno)

31st – Fish festival (Porto Cesareo)

June

9th – Cavallo Parato: in commemoration of the Crusaders of the Middle Ages, a colourful horse procession travels through the city (Brindisi)

13th – spectacular fireworks light up the skies for the Sant'Antonio festival (Vieste)

29th – a wonderful opportunity to see the frenetic and hysterical Tarantella dance (*see p17*) during the town's San Pietro e Paolo festival (Galatina)

July

2nd – the Madonna della Bruna festival is one of the liveliest of Puglia's events (Matera)

20th – a water-based *palio* competition between the different *contrade* (districts) of the town (Taranto)

24th–26th – Santa Cristina Festival boat race (Gallipoli)

30th – a celebration of the local sausage (Putignano)

July–August

In late July and early August, a series of concerts and other cultural events is held in Martina Franca and Taranto as part of the Valle d'Itria festival.

August

Throughout August Grottaglie displays its famous ceramics (*see p111*), Taranto celebrates the area's Greek heritage with a series of plays, and San Giovanni Rotondo plays host to a folk festival.

8th–11th – a medieval fair is held in the Old Town (Oria)

16th – during the San Rocco festival, competitions are held for the best fireworks display (Locorotondo)

18th – Puglia's most famous *palio* (*see p79*) (Oria)

24th–26th – the city's patron saints (Oronzo, Giusto and Fortunato) are honoured in this spectacle of lights, fireworks and local food (Lecce)

September

3rd–4th – a flotilla of boats around the port celebrates the festival of San Teodoro and San Lorenzo (Brindisi)

7th – the Madonna delle Grazie festival is celebrated with local wine and bread (Galatone)

13th–22nd – The *Disfida di Barletta* is a re-enactment of the historic battle between the French and Italians in the 16th century at which the latter were victorious (*see p48*) (Barletta)

November

1st–2nd – All Saints' Day and All Souls' Day are commemorated with bonfires (Orsara)

9th–11th – a procession and an enormous fireworks display for the festival of San Trifone (Bari)

December

5th–6th – fish and chestnuts are celebrated at the start of the Christmas period (Molfetta)

13th–24th – celebration of the local craft of papier mâché (*see p83*) with puppets and *presepe* (Nativity figures) (Lecce)

24th – Nativity plays take place around the region

Highlights

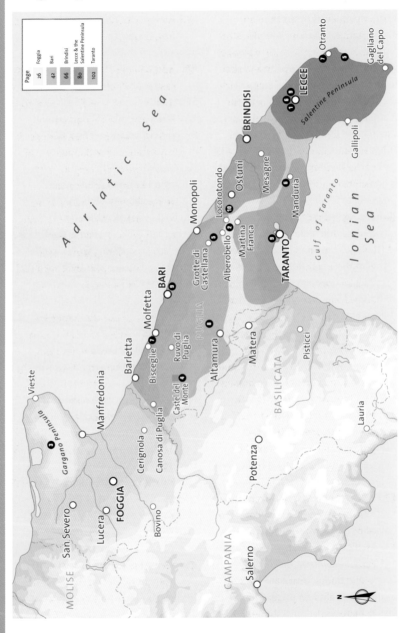

❶ Marvelling at the Baroque splendour of Lecce This is the jewel in Puglia's crown in an architectural sense. Few places on earth can boast such an explosion of Baroque imagination and skill in such a small area. Lecce's *centro storico* (historic centre) is awash with churches adorned with carved figures, saints and gargoyles, the supreme example being the façade of the Basilica di Santa Croce and the Duomo complex (*see pp84–5*).

❷ Losing yourself among the iconic *trulli* in the Valle d'Itria The Itria Valley is a wondrous area dotted with those most distinctive of Puglian houses – the *trulli* – small, domed, circular homes that have covered this landscape for centuries. For the most authentic experience, drive between the towns of Locorotondo, Cisternino and Martina Franca, deep among the olive groves and vineyards. However, to see the most *trulli* all in one place, the UNESCO-protected town of Alberobello (*see p62*) is the place to visit.

❸ Hiking in the Gargano Peninsula The best place for nature lovers in all of Puglia is the northern headland of the Gargano Peninsula. Inland this is a mountainous, protected forest of ancient oaks and pines, with numerous marked walking trails.

Along the coast are dramatic cliffs and small fishing villages (many now given over to tourism) lapped by the Adriatic (*see pp36–7*).

❹ Admiring the imposing medieval castles of Puglia A significant feature in many of Puglia's towns is the presence of dramatic defensive castles. Their existence is largely due to the domination of Frederick II in the region in the 13th century, and the area's vulnerability to invasions from both northern Italy and the Near East. The most striking castle, Castel del Monte, stands alone atop a hill as a beacon of medieval power (*see pp49–51*).

❺ Exploring beneath the earth's surface Puglia has an enormous network of caves and grottoes, many of which were discovered by archaeologists in the 19th and early 20th centuries when excavations produced evidence of Palaeolithic and Neolithic life. Among the most spectacular for its array of stalagmites and stalactites is the Grotte di Castellana (*see p62*) near Bari, as well as the cave grottoes along the coast in the Salentine Peninsula.

❻ Seeing ancient civilisations brought to life Puglia has always been a land of incomers, and many areas still bear evidence of different groups of settlers. The ancient walls of Manduria (*see p107*) are the finest remains from the Messapian era around the 3rd century BC, and numerous Roman remains have been unearthed from the time of the great empire, notably in amphitheatres such as that at Lecce (*see p81*). The Greek presence in the region is still felt in Grecia-Salentina (*see p94*), where road signs greet you in both languages.

7 **Windsurfing off two shores** Puglia is surrounded by coastline on three sides, with the Adriatic Sea in the east and the Ionian Sea in the west. Unsurprisingly, therefore, this is an ideal area for watersports. You can windsurf and kite-ski in towns such as Otranto, or simply mess about on the water, leaving from one of the many marinas at towns like Molfetta and Bisceglie.

8 **Experiencing a gastronome's delight** The whole of Italy is known for its sublime cuisine, but within that remit each area has its own specialities and Puglia is no exception. *Orecchiette* (literally, 'little ears') are the traditional pasta shapes produced here, but other highlights include *burrata* cheese, which originated from the Murgia, and, of course, superb seafood. The wine is also

surprisingly good given the extremely low prices, and the olive oil produced here is among the best (*see pp72–3*).

9 **Stumbling across archaeological treasures** Probably the best museum in the region is Taranto's Archaeological Museum (*see p103*), a veritable treasure trove of excavated finds from around the region. Lecce and Bari also have excellent museums dedicated to the region's past.

10 **Discovering the *città bianche*** The 'white towns' of Ostuni, Cisternino and Locorotondo, among others, immediately bring to mind the sun-baked villages of the Greek islands, even if they are some way from the sea. Whitewashed buildings with colourful shutters cram together in labyrinthine alleyways, adorned with pots of geraniums and the comforting aroma of home cooking, with the sounds of family life coming from behind open windows and doors.

Natural arch on the Gargano Peninsula

Suggested itineraries

Weekend

The most obvious and pleasurable place to visit in Puglia for a weekend trip is Lecce. Flights from London Stansted to Bari or, more conveniently, Brindisi are only just over two hours, with a short train ride to Lecce, leaving plenty of time to explore the city for the weekend. On arrival, head straight to the *centro storico* (old town) for a meal, and have a drink in one of the many bars that line the Via Federico d'Aragona, taking in the atmosphere of the evening *passeggiata* (stroll) and the lively buzz of this elegant town. On Saturday morning, enjoy some retail therapy before the long siesta period – either explore the many papier-mâché shops or buy some souvenir foodstuffs such as olive oil and *orecchiette* pasta

on sale in stores such as Il Borgo del Nonno (*Via V Fazzi*) near the amphitheatre on Piazza San'Oronzo. The rest of the weekend can simply be devoted to strolling the many squares, streets and alleyways of the old town, and marvelling at the Baroque splendour that has given this city its justified fame, in particular, the Duomo complex and the Basilica di Santa Croce (*see pp84–5*). If the sheer abundance of architecture gets too much, the botanical gardens beside the castle offer a tranquil and beautiful respite.

One week

For a combined city and beach break, visit Lecce and then head south to Gallipoli, where modern commercial activity combines with a traditional

Gallipoli's castle fortress

Papier-mâché figures in Lecce

fishing village atmosphere all set around a coastal castle fortress. The sandy beaches here and around the town are some of the best in Puglia, and the seafood restaurants offer the freshest of produce cooked to perfection. If you're in any doubt, pay a morning call to the fish market (*see p98*) to ogle at the variety and quality of the sea's offerings. If you travel westwards, Porto Cesareo is a popular summer resort area, complete with water parks, nightlife and fine restaurants. Alternatively, explore the eastern Salentine coast in towns such as Otranto and Santa Cesarea Terme, and take a boat trip to the magical Grotta

Zinzulusa cave. In high summer, the Torre dell'Orso resort and the Alimini Lakes just north of Otranto also offer ample sunbathing and relaxation time.

Two weeks

Nobody should miss two of the most distinctive aspects of the Puglia region: the *trulli* houses of the Valle d'Itria (*see pp64–5*) and the hilltop *città bianche* (white towns) nearby. Of all the white towns, Ostuni is the most charming; it is almost as if a Greek Cyclades island village has been picked up brick by brick and set down in this sunny Italian location. Wander the steep cobbled lanes lined with whitewashed houses and window boxes of blooming geraniums, stop for refreshment at one of the numerous elegant bars and cafés, and take in the views from the summit of the town. Travelling west, Cisternino and Locorotondo offer similar experiences on an altogether smaller and more intimate scale. For more Baroque flamboyance, visit the small historic centre (*centro storico*) of Martina Franca, with its striking cathedral. Alberobello is a town of note because it has the largest collection of *trulli* houses, those intriguing squat buildings topped with conical roofs, but there's also a bit of a tourist overkill. The drive through the valley in this region offers the most beautiful landscape, the houses seemingly placed at random, in varying degrees of repair, amid swathes of olive groves and vineyards. From here, it's just a short distance to the Grotte di Castellana (*see p62*), one of the most impressive cave complexes in Europe. Going south, there are two options: for nature lovers, the rocky villages west of Taranto offer one of the most memorable natural landscapes in Puglia; for urbanites, Taranto's new town is a sophisticated retail area, even if its old town is now sadly in dire need of repair.

Longer

Continuing westwards, the city of Bari is very much a commercial port, but it is worth a short visit for its evocative Old Town. The harbour-front towns of Molfetta, Barletta and particularly Trani, with its stunning waterside cathedral, all warrant a stop for their architecture and landscape. Castel del Monte is another unmissable highlight of Puglia, marking Frederick II's most powerful addition to a landscape already dominated by his insatiable love for defensive fortresses (*see pp49–51*). Archaeology buffs will want to see the remains of Canne destroyed by Hannibal and the Carthaginians and now preserved as a historic site (*see p47*). From here, it's an easy drive to the natural gem of Puglia, the Gargano Peninsula (*see pp36–7*), where fishing villages and small tourist resorts sit in the sunny shadow of the promontory, atop of which is the Umbra Forest, now a designated national park and a wonderful area for hiking.

Typical *trulli* can be seen all across the region

Foggia

The province of Foggia is the gateway to the Puglia region from the north of Italy, sharing its border with Campania. The landscape is largely dominated by the grid-like tavoliere *plain (literally 'tableland') where fields of wheat have been cultivated for centuries. The importance of this can be seen in the main town, Foggia, whose name derives from* fovea *(ditch), referring to the underground wheat stores. The region is also the most industrial in Puglia.*

The region has one of the most stunning coastal routes in Puglia, with the Gargano Peninsula jutting out like an upturned thumb, combining both traditional fishing villages, tourist coast resorts and a beautiful inland forest that

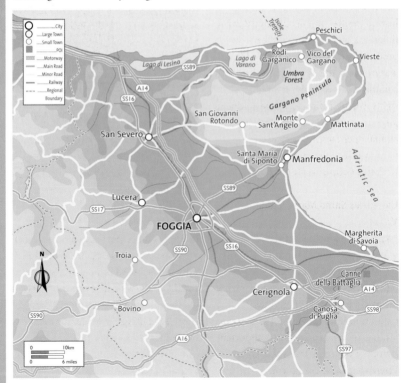

now has national park status. Other highlights include the castles dating from the time of Frederick II (*see p51*), beautiful churches and cathedrals and, for wine lovers, the famous vines of San Severo. A wonderful offshore excursion is to take the ferry from the Gargano Peninsula to the Isole Tremiti, which have long been an Italian secret of azure waters and pine forests.

Foggia

Two main tragedies have befallen Foggia, the provincial capital – an earthquake in the 18th century and World War II. As a result, very little remains of what was once a fine historic centre, populated since Roman times and trading on the wheat produced in the surrounding fields. Nevertheless, this is a pleasant if slightly commercial town, with a number of sights worth visiting. If you're an opera lover, try to visit in autumn when an annual opera festival is staged in honour of Foggia's native composer Umberto Giordano (1867–1948).

Cattedrale Santa Maria Icona Vetere

Foggia's Romanesque cathedral originally dates from the latter half of the 12th century, but much of it was renovated in the 18th century following the earthquake of 1731, and the renovation brought with it the Baroque features of the day. The most important feature of the cathedral is the Icona Vetere chapel, where an icon of the

Ancient, narrow street in Vieste, Foggia

Virgin Mary dating from the 11th century is on display – legend has it that the icon was discovered in swampland by some shepherd boys who saw three small flames rising up from the water. On the cathedral façade, much of the cornice detailing can be attributed to the influence of Frederick II.

Via Duomo. No telephone. Open: daily. Free admission.

The Galleria Provincial d'Arte Moderna at Palazzo Dogana

PADRE PIO

One of the most famous religious figures of 20th-century Italy is the Puglia-born Capuchin priest known as Padre Pio (1887–1968). Born Francesco Forgione, his first calling was in Foggia, but it was during his second posting in 1918 in San Giovanni Rotondo that his fame was assured. On 20 September of that year, after the celebrations of the Feast of the Stigmata of St Francis, Padre Pio was found wailing in pain, with blood oozing out of his hands and feet in the exact same spots that Jesus had suffered during the Crucifixion. Padre Pio would continue to bleed, off and on, from these points for the rest of his life. From then on, he was venerated and held responsible for a wide range of miracles and healings, although not everyone was so convinced of his gifts – Pope Pius XI viewed him with suspicion and barred him from preaching. Twenty-four years after his death, however, Padre Pio was canonised as St Pio of Pietrelcina by Pope John Paul II, and San Giovanni Rotondo has become a mass pilgrimage site for those followers of Padre Pio's cult.

Chiesa delle Croci

At the end of the 17th century, a Capuchin monk visited Foggia and planted seven crosses here, and within a few years this became the site of the five-chapelled church, notable for its triumphal arch and Baroque detailing. During the 19th century, the church's crypt was one of the many secret meeting places for the Risorgimento – the campaigning group that sought to unify the nation – that were set up around the country.
Piazza Sant'Eligio. No telephone.
Open: daily. Free admission.

Museo Civico

The area around Foggia has long been the focus of archaeological excavations, and many of the finds are displayed in this former palazzo. The museum is also home to an art gallery (*pinacoteca*) with works by artists of the 19th and 20th centuries and a folk art collection.
Piazza V Nigri 1. Tel: (0881) 726245.
Open: Tue–Sun 9am–1pm, 4–7pm
(9am–1pm only Wed & Sat).
Admission charge.

Palazzo Dogana

One of the most significant chapters in Foggia's history was during its role as headquarters for *la transumanza* (migration) of sheep from the Abruzzi mountains to the *tavoliere* plains. Each year, the shepherds would lead their flocks across designated grassy tracks of pastureland down to the plains. In the 15th century, it was decided that a tax would be levied on this vital process to boost the riches of the Neapolitan king, who was, at the time, in charge of the region. The Palazzo Dogana was the Customs House where this tax had to be paid. Today, the Baroque building is home to the provincial administrative offices as well as the Galleria Provincial d'Arte Moderna (Modern Art Gallery).
Piazza XX Settembre.
Tel: (0881) 791111.
Open: daily 8am–2pm, 3.30–7pm.
Free admission.

Operatic characters in Piazza Giordano

Piazza Giordano

Foggia's native composer, Umberto Giordano, is honoured in this small eponymous square on the main drag towards the cathedral. At the centre of the square is a statue of the great musician, while surrounding him are further statues depicting characters from his operas such as *Andria Chenier*, *Fedora*, *Il Re* and *Siberia*.

Bovino

The small town of Bovino is often overlooked by tourists but it's well worth a brief stop, particularly for its impressive cathedral, important castle and medieval centre. Surrounded by hills, olive groves and vineyards, the landscape is one of the most picturesque in the area.

Basilica Concattedrale (Cathedral)

The town's main site is the Romanesque-Byzantine cathedral in the heart of the *centro storico* (historic centre), dating from the 11th century. The façade is decorated with various floral stone reliefs, but the most dominant feature is the rose window above the main entrance, at the centre of which is the figure of Christ the Pantocrator. The window is a replacement of the original, which was destroyed during an earthquake in 1930.

The interior takes the form of a Latin cross and is notable for its stone Corinthian and Ionic columns and a stone baptismal font decorated with reliefs of deer, doves and griffins, among other scenes. The high wall is dominated by the organ pipes, while below are choir stalls dating from the early 17th century. There's also a stairway from the transept to the Chapel of San Marco, and the chapel is decorated with a lovely Baroque altar.
Via San Marco 1. Tel: (0881) 966236. Open: daily. Free admission.

Castello Ducale (Ducal Castle)

For centuries, the area around Bovino was renowned for bandits who attacked those making the treacherous journey between Campania and the Adriatic. During the occupation of Frederick II, it was decided that a defensive castle was required, and the original ornamentations and round tower can still be seen dominating the area.

The castle retained its defensive role in this difficult region over the centuries, but it was also converted into a ducal residence of various important dynasties, among them the Angevins. The castle was embellished with details such as a clock tower and a hanging garden. The interior of the castle is now open to the public, and the lavishness of the furnishings befits the wealth of those who resided here, while the chapel is distinguished by its mosaic floor and a supposed fragment of Christ's Crown of Thorns.
Via Castello. Tel: (0881) 912015. Open: Mon–Fri 10am–12.30pm & 4–7pm. Free admission.

Troia

This rather windswept, hilltop town, peering down over the *tavoliere* plains,

may not, at first sight, have much to offer visitors and, indeed, locals appear somewhat nonplussed by their presence. However, there are several ancient churches, a museum documenting the town's history, and its most important sight, the cathedral.

Cattedrale (Cathedral)

Completed in the first quarter of the 12th century, the more striking elements of the Romanesque façade are the rose window and the mix-and-match architectural details of the reliefs that combine northern Italian styles with Byzantine. Inside, highlights include the heavily decorated columns and a treasury of religious artefacts.
Via Duomo. No telephone. Open: daily. Free admission.

The Romanesque cathedral in Troia

Lucera

Possibly the most historic town in the province, many rulers have fought over and governed Lucera down the centuries, including Emperor Augustus and Frederick II. The latter defined the town by constructing one of his Puglian castles which looms over Lucera from its hilltop location. Today, the *centro storico* (old town) is a wonderfully atmospheric maze of narrow cobbled lanes overhung with balconies and the ubiquitous laundry blowing in the breeze.

Anfiteatro Romano Augusteo (Roman Amphitheatre)

Just outside the town are the remains of the largest Roman amphitheatre in southern Italy, which were uncovered

Lucera's pretty cathedral

in the 1930s and date from the time of Augustus. The vast arena that could accommodate just under 20,000 spectators goes some way to illustrating how significant this town was during Roman times. The most impressive surviving features today are the two large gateways decorated with Ionic columns and a stone relief of a shield and spear indicating the gladiatorial battles that would have taken place here. Other areas related to the games can still be made out, including the competitors' dressing areas, the lines around the arena where barriers would have separated the audience and performers, and an underground area where the animals would have been housed.

Viale Augusteo. Tel: (0881) 522762. Open daily 9am–2pm. Free admission.

Anfiteatro Romano Augusteo

Cattedrale dell'Assunta

During Frederick II's rule of the town, the predominant religion of his Saracen troops was Islam. Yet when Charles of Anjou took over in 1269, Christianity was restored. To this aim, the cathedral was built in the Gothic style popular at the turn of the 14th century, and with definitive French influences. Its rose-pink stone, offset by white borders around portal and windows, dominates the small square on which it stands. So important is the cathedral to the region – one of the finest Puglian-style edifices – that it was declared a national monument in the 19th century just after Unification. Among its highlights

are the vast apse, the vaulted ceilings, the baptistery sheltered by a cupola, and a 15th-century fresco depicting the *Pietà*. Although not proven, it is thought that some aspects of the altar were brought here from the castle northwest of the town where Frederick II breathed his last, such as his extravagant stone dining table.

Piazza Duomo. Tel: (800) 767606. Open: Apr–Sept 8am–noon & 5–8pm; Oct–Mar 8am–noon & 4–7pm. Free admission.

Fortezza Svevo-Angioina

You can't miss Lucera's most famous sight. Its 24 towers and surrounding wall stretching for 1km (²/₃ mile) bear down on the town from their hilltop position as they have done since they were built in 1233. Built on the site of a former Roman acropolis by Frederick II, the castle was later modified by Charles of Anjou, to whom the defensive wall can be credited. The current iron bridge, replacing a wooden original, dates from 2000.

Piazza Padre Angelo. Open: Apr–Oct Tue–Sun 9am–2pm & 3–6pm (Sat & Sun mornings only); Nov–Mar Tue–Sun 9am–2pm. Free admission.

Museo Civico Giuseppe Fiorelli

Roman finds that have been excavated in the area are on display in the town's museum set in a 17th-century former *palazzo*. Among the ancient exhibits are mosaic tiling thought to have come from nearby thermal baths, and coins and ceramics. There are also more recent glories that were mainly used by the aristocratic families of the area, including a 17th-century crib, Venetian chandeliers, and works by local artists of the 19th century.

Via de'Nicastri. Tel: (800) 547041. Open: Oct–Mar Tue–Sat 9am–1pm & 3.30–6.30pm, Sun 9am–1pm; Apr–Sept Tue–Sat 9am–1pm & 4–7pm, Sun 9am–1pm. Admission charge.

San Severo

Legend has it that the ancient town of San Severo was founded by the Greek god Diomedes. Whatever the real story, it has been a thriving centre ever since. Today, the town is best known for its production of the dry white wine San Severino, but its church is well worth a visit for its Romanesque details and its beautiful rose window.

Isole Tremiti

Just over 20km (12 miles) off the Gargano coast, the four Tremiti Islands (San Nicola, San Domino, Pianosa and Capraia) are a lovely getaway of limestone cliffs and secluded bays. Snorkellers and divers abound here, coming to view sea life such as sea urchins, lobster, cuttlefish and conger eels.

San Domino is most popular with tourists because of its beach and accommodation facilities, but San Nicola is of more interest if you want more than sea and sand. The island's abbey, Santa Maria e Mare, was founded by Benedictine monks from Montecassino in the early 11th century. However, the position was always vulnerable and the monks were eventually massacred by invading pirates in the 14th century.

Over the centuries, the abbey was occupied by other religious factions who made various additions to the building, but in the 18th century Ferdinand IV of Naples converted the abbey into a prison, a role continued until 1945.

The layout of the original interior can still be seen, but many of the other details date from later periods, such as the 15th-century portal.

Margherita di Savoia

The area around this coastal town is best known for its salt flats (*see p41*) that cast a lovely rosy glow over the area as the sun reflects on the white of the mineral. A museum in the town is dedicated to the traditions of salt mining, which has been a thriving industry here as far back as the 3rd century BC and is now the most essential in Italy.

Museo Storico Archeologico Industriale della Salina. Corso Vittorio Emanuele. Tel: (0883) 657519. www.museosalina.it. Open: Jul–Sept daily 7–11pm, Oct–Jun Mon–Fri 10am–noon. Free admission.

View from San Domino, Isole Tremiti

Drive: Gargano Peninsula and Umbra Forest

The hilly, forested Gargano Peninsula, now a designated national park area, is in stark contrast to the wheat fields of the tavoliere, and offers a breathtaking drive of sea views and charming fishing villages. In an otherwise flat area of Italy, the Gargano Peninsula is a welcome contrast as the roads weave around the foothills, amid a sea of olive groves and almond trees.

The 160km (100-mile) route is accessed via the SS89. It could be completed in around 4 hours, but given the winding coastal road and sights along the way, you should allow a full day.

1 Lago di Lesina

Cut off from the Adriatic by a series of sand dunes and woodland, this lake is an ideal place to begin your drive of the peninsula. The town of Lesina dates from the Middle Ages, and there are a few churches of this period. It is also home to the visitors' centre of the Gargano National Park where you can pick up information about the region. *Continue for 50km (31 miles) on SS89 to Rodi Garganico.*

2 Rodi Garganico

Don't let the apartment blocks that greet you at the entrance to this town,

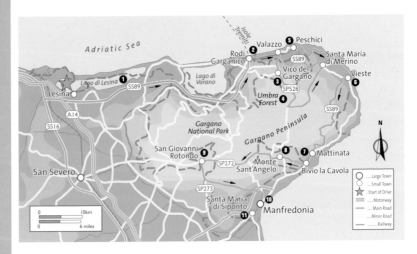

The waterfront at Vieste

today the main centre of the peninsula, put you off. Nearer the sea, the evocative alleyways of this ancient fishing village, filled with faded pastel-coloured houses with wrought-iron balconies, make for a lovely stroll, and the views out to sea with the aroma of citrus trees and the squawks of swifts and gulls filling the air should not be missed. In addition, there's a lovely sandy beach that is good for families. This is also the port for ferries to the Isole Tremiti (*see p34*).
Drive 6km (4 miles) on SS89 to Valazzo, then take the SP528 5km (3 miles) to Vico del Gargano.

3 Vico del Gargano

The production of citrus fruits, as well as olives, is important in this small

inland town, but its main feature is the castle, one of the many constructed by Frederick II. A peculiar tradition of the town is to give your loved one fruit on St Valentine's Day in the so-called *vicolo del bacio* (alleyway of the kiss).
Continue 10km (6 miles) along the SP528 into the centre of the Umbra Forest.

4 Foresta Umbra (Umbra Forest)

The only true forested area in Puglia and now protected as a national park, the Umbra Forest makes for a wonderful nature experience.
The landscaped paths and cycle tracks wind through beech, pine, maple and chestnut trees, while wildlife includes deer, rabbit and wild foxes.

In the centre of the forest is the **Rifugio Foresta Umbra** (*Open: Apr–Oct*), which offers explanations about the landscape and its history. *Follow the signs for Santa Maria di Merino for approximately 15km (9 miles) then head west on the SS89 to Peschici.*

5 Peschici

Few places along the peninsula offer such wonderful views as the clifftop town of Peschici, although the switchback roads to the beach are not for the faint-hearted. Within the town itself there is a castle and a medieval church, but the most pleasant activity is simply to walk around the whitewashed alleyways.
Continue along the coast road for 30km (18 miles) to Vieste, bearing in mind that the winding route will take longer than you might expect.

6 Vieste

The most important resort on the peninsula because of its expansive sandy beaches and accommodation options, Vieste is also of significant historical importance. Inhabited since Roman times, present features include an 11th-century cathedral and castle, and the *chiang amer* (bitter stone), purportedly the site where the town's old and infirm were murdered by Turkish pirates in the mid-16th century. In fact, the town is largely split in two between the 'old' town of the Middle Ages and the 'new' town that mainly dates from the 18th century.

Aside from its sandy bays, the coastline here is distinguished by the 26m (85ft) -high limestone pinnacle known as Pizzomunnu that stands isolated a few metres from the mainland like a cast-aside friend. It's also possible to see local fishermen seeking their catch from *trabucchi* (traditional pinewood poles).
Take the SS89 south for 30km (18 miles) to Mattinata.

7 Mattinata

The town of Mattinata is set slightly away from the sea on an inland hillside location. This gives the Mattinata Lido and the town's small marina a wonderful mountain backdrop, even if the coastline changes from sand to pebbles here. The area with its caves eroded into the coastal cliffs will appeal to spelaeologists. Just outside of the town, there are remains of a necropolis dating from the 7th century BC. Food lovers should take the opportunity to buy local almonds and figs in season, which are the mainstay of the local economy.
Continue along the SS89 to Bivio la Cavola, then take the SP272 turn 10km (6 miles) inland to Monte Sant'Angelo.

8 Monte Sant'Angelo

Most visitors to the Gargano Peninsula today come for the views and the beaches, but the area has been a pilgrimage site since a 5th-century bishop claimed to have had visions of the Archangel Michael. In response to this, a sanctuary was constructed in honour of the saint, and pilgrims began following the route between here and the related Mont Saint Michel in France. The grotto in the centre of the town around which it was built can still be visited, down a steep staircase accessed through a Gothic doorway, but the statue of San Michele is not the original, and dates from the 16th century.

Santuario di San Michele. Tel: (0884) 561150. Open: Apr–Sept 7am–8pm; Oct–Mar 7.30am–12.30pm & 2.30–5pm. Admission charge.
Continue along the SP272 for 20km (12 miles) to San Giovanni Rotondo.

9 San Giovanni Rotondo

Another important pilgrimage site, this small town is renowned as the parish and burial place of Padre Pio (*see p29*), housed in a purpose-built

church designed by acclaimed architect Renzo Piano.
Head south on the SP273, then follow the signs to Manfredonia for 13km (8 miles).

10 Manfredonia

The largest town on the Gargano Peninsula is now largely industrial and, at first sight, extremely unattractive. However, the town was established in the Middle Ages and a few remnants of that era can still be seen, in particular the **Castello Svevo-Angioino**, which is now home to an archaeological museum detailing the history of the region. Also of note is the 17th-century cathedral that was built as a return to Catholic rule after the town had fallen to the Turks some 60 years before.

Museo Archeologico Nazionale del Gargano. Via Castello Svevo. Tel: (0884) 538831. Open: 8.30am–7.30pm. Admission charge.
Continue along the SS89 for 4km (2½ miles) to Santa Maria di Siponto.

11 Santa Maria di Siponto

The ancient Roman town of Sipontum was destroyed by an earthquake in 1223 and by an ensuing malaria epidemic. Yet the beautiful 12th-century cathedral Santa Maria di Siponto survived, today protected from the main road by gated walls. The mixture of Romanesque and Byzantine details clearly illustrates the conflicting influences at play in the area at the time.

The golden stonework of Santa Maria di Siponto

Puglian wildlife

In a region where the land is very much a working agricultural necessity, there has not been a long tradition of preserving wildlife environments in ecological terms. However, this is slowly beginning to change as environmentalists are taking note of some of Puglia's important natural habitats.

The Gargano Peninsula (*see pp36–9*) is Puglia's only national park, established in 1995. At its heart is the Umbra Forest, with approximately 11,000ha (27,200 acres) of shady lanes and dense woodlands dotted with Aleppo pines, chestnut trees, beeches and ancient oaks – some of the latter can claim to be more than 2,000 years old. The forest is also known for its extensive species of orchids, as well as many other woodland flowers such as anemones and peonies. In terms of fauna, the forest is a natural habitat for deer,

Pines populate the Gargano Peninsula

Wild crocuses blooming in autumn

foxes, badgers and even wild cats, while its varied birdlife includes cuckoos, doves and hawks.

Not far from the Gargano Peninsula is the vast area of salt pans near the town of Margherita di Savoia (*see pp34–5*). Producing as much as 700,000 tonnes of salt per year, the area is a mainstay of the local economy, but in terms of wildlife its wetlands (6,000ha/14,800 acres) have been drawing ornithologists for years – even Frederick II was known to have made notes on the avian population here in the Middle Ages. The most notable inhabitants are herons and

flamingos, but the area is also home to coots, sheldrakes, avocets, falcons and more.

In the Salento region, in the far south of Puglia, the Alimini Lakes (*see p91*) are a lush area of reeds and pine trees, while within the waters carp and mullet are among the fish that thrive here. On the opposite side of the coastline is an area known as Porto Selvaggio (literally 'wild port'), an area of cliffs and *macchia* (scrubland) that is protected against tourist development and is home to lizards, weasels and finches.

Bari

One of the gateways to southern Italy and an important trading port from ancient times to the present day, the city of Bari is imperative to the economy of the Puglia region, even if it is not the most attractive city outside its old town quarter. The region surrounding Bari, however, is extremely rich in places to see and visit and will satisfy all manner of interests.

Frederick II put his stamp on the region, as he did with the rest of Puglia, with his many castles demonstrating his imperial power, including the most striking of all, the mysterious Castel del Monte. Both the Middle Ages and later Baroque embellishments make the many churches and cathedrals places worthy of veneration as well as worship. The countryside, long an important agricultural region, is dotted with not only kilometre upon kilometre of olive groves but also with ancient megaliths and quaint *trulli* (*see pp64–5*), while cave systems such as the spectacular Grotte di Castellana are some of the most important in Europe.

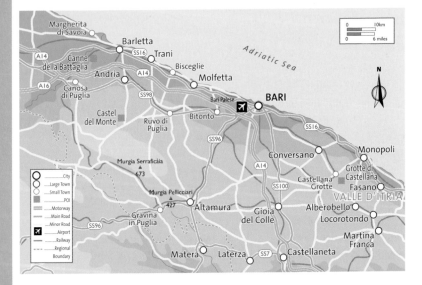

Bari

In administrative terms, Bari is the capital of Puglia, and its coastal location has given it an unequalled importance – this is the point on the Italian mainland from which the Crusaders departed to the Middle East, and over the centuries, the Greeks, Romans, Lombards and Normans have all staked a claim to the strategic city. The town is still a bustling ferry port, with boats departing to Greece, Albania and Croatia, but, as can be seen from the coastal skyline, it's also a highly industrial area, and this adds to a rather grimy atmosphere. As a result, there is little to attract the visitor to the New Town area other than two museums of note.

Museo Archeologico Provinciale

The close links between Greece and southern Italy in ancient times can be clearly seen in this archaeological museum with its plentiful array of vases and coins from both regions. Also on display is a range of bronzes, jewellery and ceramics excavated from sites in the region such as Bitonto (*see p59*) and Canne della Battaglia (*see p47*).
Palazzo dell'Ateneo, Piazza Umberto 1. Tel: (080) 5412422. Closed for renovation.

Pinacoteca Provinciale

Housed in 16 rooms in the uppermost floor of a former *palazzo*, this is one of the most significant art museums in the

Boats in the harbour at Bari

region. The collection covers local artworks from the medieval period to the 20th century. Many of the earlier works and fragments of architectural details were brought here from churches around the province and across southern Italy. A number of important art periods and schools are represented, including Renaissance, rococo and works from Venice and Naples.
Palazzo della Provincia, Lungomare N Sauro. Tel: (080) 5412421. Open: Tue–Sat 9am–7pm, Sun 9am–3pm. Admission charge.

Walk: Bari Old Town

The change between Bari's New Town and the Città Vecchia (Old Town) occurs at the broad strip that is Corso Vittorio Libertà Emanuele. North of here you leave behind the orderly grid-like streets of the modern town and immerse yourself in the meandering, shady alleyways of days gone by.

The walk covers approximately 1km (²⁄₃ mile) and, with stops, can be completed in 2–3 hours.

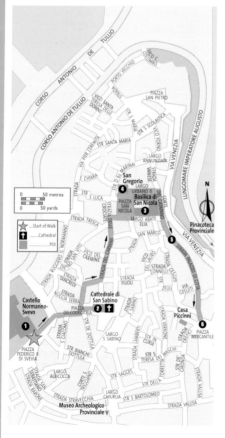

1 Castello Normanno-Svevo

Start your walk at the main sight of the Old Town, the imposing 13th-century castle built during the occupation of Frederick II and later embellished in the 16th century by Isabel of Aragon. What was once a moat to detract potential invaders is now a slightly ramshackle garden planted with palm trees, which gives the castle a more attractive setting than many of its more austere counterparts. Inside, the main point of interest for visitors is the Gipsoteca del Castello, a large hall housing copies of Romanesque architecture from around the region.

Piazza Federico II di Svevia 4. Tel: (080) 5286111. Open: Tue–Sun 9am–1pm, 3.30–7pm (9am–1pm only Sun). Admission charge.
From the Piazza Federico II di Svevia, head one block northeast to Piazza dell'Odegitria and the cathedral.

2 Cattedrale di San Sabino

Romanesque meets Byzantine meets Baroque on the façade of Bari's impressive cathedral, named after the city's first patron saint. The interior, however, is true to its 12th-century origins, even if some aspects, such as the pulpit, are merely copies of earlier works. It was long believed that the cathedral was constructed over the ruins of a former church, a fact that has now been revealed by the uncovering of 8th-century mosaics beneath the floor. Attached to the cathedral, housed in the archbishop's palace, is a museum that displays and preserves ecclesiastical relics and artworks from various centuries.
Piazza dell'Odegitria. Museum: Tel: (080) 5210605. Open: Thur & Sun 9.30am–12.30pm, Sat 9.30am–12.30pm & 4.30–7.30pm. Free admission.

Head north along Strada del Carmine then Strada delle Crociate to Piazza San Nicola and the basilica.

3 Basilica di San Nicola

The most important religious building in Bari is not, in fact, the cathedral but this church to St Nicholas – among the first Norman churches in southern Italy, dating from 1087. Its vast gabled and arched façade, flanked by sturdy square towers, shows much in common with other Norman architecture in the region, although this is more clearly seen in castles than in churches. The church is of major importance during the festival of St Nicholas when, on 6 December and 9 May, a statue of the saint is carried here in a procession. As if the dominance of the church were not enough to illustrate the importance

Walk: Bari Old Town

Castello Normanno-Svevo

of St Nicholas to the city, an arch in front of the church displays a stone carving of him.

Piazza San Nicola.
www.basilicasannicola.it.
Open: 7.30am–1pm & 4–7.30pm.
Free admission.
With your back to the basilica, head to the right-hand corner of the piazza to the church of San Gregorio.

4 San Gregorio

When the statue of St Nicholas is not residing in its basilica on festival days, it is to be found in this simple 11th-century church.

Piazza San Nicola. Open: 7.30am–1pm & 4–7.30pm. Free admission.
Walk along the side of Basilica di San Nicola along Largo Urbano II and around the back on Corte del Catapano and into Strada Palazzo di Città.

5 Strada Palazzo di Città

This street is so-named because it was home to various *palazzi* during the 16th century, but today it has an altogether more workaday feel. Amid the boutiques and cafés that now occupy the former grand buildings, you'll see Bari life in all its relaxed ease – don't be surprised to see local *mamme* sitting on steps making home-made pasta for their families' evening meals, exchanging the day's gossip as they work.

Walk to the end of the street and enter the Piazza Mercantile.

6 Piazza Mercantile

The heart of Bari's Old Town is this large, bustling square, once the political centre of the town in the Middle Ages and now home to the Town Hall, the city council and a 19th-century fish market that is due for renovation. The square is a good place to end your walk, and you can take refreshment at one of the parasol-covered café tables. As befits its name, there is still a daily market here. The square is also the location of the entrance to the Casa Piccinni, the birthplace of the Bari-born composer Niccolò Piccinni (1728–1800), which houses a museum examining his life. Concerts are held here on a regular basis.

Casa Piccinni. Vico Fiscardi 2.
Tel: (080) 5214561. Open: 10am–noon.
Admission charge.
To return to the New Town, head south on Strada Orefici to Piazza del Ferrarese and south again to Piazza IV Novembre.

The façade of Bari's cathedral

View across to Bari Old Town

Canne della Battaglia

While the Roman army was rarely
seriously threatened at the height of its
reign, one such incident occurred
during the Punic Wars between Rome
and Carthage. In 216 BC, that great
warrior Hannibal and his Carthaginian
troops managed to inflict serious
damage on the area known as Cannae,
virtually levelling the town and killing a
large proportion of its inhabitants.

Today, the battle site is protected as
an archaeological zone known as the
Antiquarium di Canne della Battaglia,
where ruins of the once noble houses as
well as various objects such as ceramics
and jewellery have been excavated.
*Antiquarium di Canne della Battaglia.
13km (8 miles) north of Canosa di
Puglia. Tel: (0883) 510992. Open: Tue–
Sun 8.30am–7.30pm. Admission charge.*

Canosa di Puglia

Of great importance to the Greeks,
Romans and the Normans because
of its strategic position, Canosa offers
yet more historical gems. A Roman
amphitheatre once stood in what are
now the town's public gardens, and its
ruined columns can still be seen, while
the **Museo Civico Archeologico
(Archaeological Museum)** houses a few
of the local red and black vases that
were renowned for their beauty and
craftsmanship.

The 11th-century cathedral was home
to the first diocese in Puglia, and its most
notable feature today is the elaborate
bishop's throne, the legs of which are
carved elephants.
*Museo Civico Archeologico. Via Terenzio
Varrone 45. Tel: (0883) 663685. Open:
Tue–Sun 9am–1pm, 4–6pm.*

The enormous *Colosso* of Barletta

Barletta

Barletta may play second fiddle to Bari now, but it has been an important town since Norman times and is still a major trade and industry centre. One of its most famous incidents in history was the *Disfidia di Barletta*, a challenge between the Italians and invading French in 1503. The Italians won, a victory that is celebrated every September when locals re-enact the event (*see p19*).

One of the symbols of Barletta is the enormous bronze *Colosso* statue on Corso Vittorio Emanuele, also known as Eracleo, so-named because it reaches a staggering height of 5m (16ft). It is supposedly cast in the image of a Roman emperor, but nobody can really decide which one.

Castello di Barletta

Yet another of Frederick II's vast castle complexes was also an important player during the Crusades, but much of what is seen from the outside today dates from reconstructions in the 15th century, including the solid and stark defensive bastions. Nevertheless, the mood is broken by the lovely garden setting, surrounded by palm trees on one side and the sea on the other.

The interior of the castle is used to house items excavated from Canne della Battaglia (*see p47*).

To add to the military atmosphere, the little 'streets' in the gardens around the castle commemorate heroes from both world wars. Piazzale 15 Maggio 1915 remembers an attack on the castle by an Austrian warship on that date, and Viale della Shoah honours the Jews who perished at the hands of the Nazis.

Piazza Castello. Tel: (0883) 578612. Open: Apr–Sept Tue–Sun 9am–1pm & 4–8pm; Oct–Mar Tue–Sun 9am–1pm & 3–7pm. Admission charge.

Chiesa di Santo Sepolcro (Church of the Holy Sepulchre)

Near the *Colosso* is Barletta's most important church dating from the 11th–13th centuries, although the façade was restored in the 18th century. The church was the seat of the Archbishop of Nazareth from 1291 to the 19th century and, as such, played an important role during the Crusades. *Corso Giuseppe Garibaldi 77. Tel: (0883) 531782. Open: 9am–noon & 4–7pm. Free admission.*

Pinacoteca Giuseppe de Nittis

Located in the Baroque Palazzo della Marra, Barletta's newest museum is dedicated to the native-born 19th-century artist who became a major figure on the Impressionist art scene in Paris. Works range from rural landscapes to cityscapes of London, and as well as more than 200 works by De Nittis there are also exhibits of his contemporaries, including Renoir. *Via Enrico Cialdini 74. Tel: (088) 538312. www.pinacotecadenittis.it. Open: Mon 10am–2pm, Tue–Thur, Sat–Sun 10am–8pm, Fri 10am–11pm. Admission charge.*

Castel del Monte

Without question, the Castel del Monte is a highlight of any trip to the entire region of Puglia. The landscape may be dotted all over with Frederick II's many castles and fortresses, but none has

Fountains at the Castello di Barletta

such a commanding position or grandeur as this one, a fact recognised by UNESCO when it granted the castle World Heritage status in 1996. The Italians themselves declared it a national monument when giving out such honours following Unification, and they set about restoring the decayed castle from 1879 through to the 1920s.

Set on a hilltop 540m (1,771ft) above sea level, one of the great charms of the complex is its successful blend of architectural styles that would, with lesser design skills, merely clash with one other. Here, however, flamboyant Moorish details seem quite at home alongside sombre Romanesque lines. Another remarkable aspect of the castle is the use of octagonal structures – from the façade to the interior, octagons exist within octagons in an ongoing theme. Many historians have associated this with a symbolism intended to illustrate Frederick's great power – the number eight is regularly

The forbidding exterior of the Castel del Monte

FREDERICK II

German by heritage and officially known as Frederick of Hohenstaufen, Frederick II (1194–1250) was the son of Constance of Altavilla, heiress of Sicily, and grandson of Frederick Barbarossa. Orphaned from the age of four, Frederick grew up under the protection of Pope Innocent III. He started exerting his power over southern Italy in 1220, soon after he ascended the Sicilian throne. He further boosted his powers by becoming Holy Roman Emperor in 1220, effectively ruling both countries, although he paid little heed to his native land. Although he spent much of his life involved with the Crusades that were an attempt to reclaim Jerusalem from the Muslims and return it to the pope, Frederick had a troubled relationship with the Papacy. In truth, his own megalomania was at odds with another ruling body. His consistent construction of castles and fortresses within southern Italy remains as lasting evidence of the importance he bestowed on his own reign and the lengths to which he would go to protect it.

Not that his interests were purely military, however – Frederick was acknowledged by all to be an extremely cultured man, with an interest in architecture, science and poetry that earned him the nickname *stupor mundi* (wonder of the world).

After Frederick's death, his son Manfred succeeded him in controlling most of the southern peninsula. Yet Manfred's inherited anti-papal attitudes incited Pope Urban IV who successfully engaged the French Charles of Anjou, very much on the side of the Vatican, to defeat him in Benevento, Campania, in 1266.

seen as symbolic of the Revelation in Christian religion (baptismal fonts, for example, are usually octagonal). Also, the eight-sided shape has been associated with labyrinths for centuries. Other suggestions are that the castle was designed in accordance with astronomy, a science that is known to have fascinated Frederick II.

Inside, there is little of material value to see apart from a few displays of ruined sculptures and columns. Yet the interior is not only worth visiting for the mastery of the architecture but also to soak up the ambience of a time and period of history, and the self-importance of the man who created it. *Via Castel del Monte, 18km (11 miles) from Andria. Tel: (080) 5286237. Open: Mar–Sept 10.15am–7.45pm; Oct–Feb 9.15am–6.45pm. Admission charge.*

The castle has a spartan interior

Puglia's castles

With its vulnerable position, surrounded by coastline on both sides and in a precarious situation between east and west, Puglia has always had to protect itself from invaders. In Roman times, fortresses were a common necessity, and the Byzantines too saw the need for defences in towns such as Troia. Yet today this history is most apparent in the castles (*castelli*) that were built during the Norman period and, in particular, during the rule of Frederick II – 29 in all. Hilltop castles, allowing far-reaching views and therefore better-prepared defence, can be seen both in coastal cities and inland. The latter, if the position was strategic enough, had the added advantage of views of both coastlines.

The *castello* at Trani, with its beautiful setting in the harbour

The design of the castles generally consisted of thick, fortified walls, with corner towers or bastions. Inside, there were vast halls, galleries and, in some cases, chapels. Most of the castles take the form of a quadrilateral or polygonal plan, apart from the finest castle in the region, Castel del Monte (*see pp49–51*), dating from 1240, which is octagonal. The reasons for this are unknown but may have been influenced by Middle Eastern architecture – Frederick II would have been a visitor to the region during the Crusades. Nevertheless, its unusual shape makes it a breathtaking monument. Other excellent examples of castle architecture can be found at Lucera (*see pp32–4*), Bari (*see pp42–6*), Barletta (*see p48*) and Trani (*see p54*), and the square solidity of the latter is beautifully reflected in the waters of the Adriatic Sea. Most castles are now open to the public as tourist sights – Taranto's castle, however, is still used for military activities.

Bari's castle ramparts

Many of the castles were later modified or expanded by ensuing leaders, specifically the Angevins and Aragonese, and in the 17th century many had Baroque elements added to their rather stark original structures. The Aragonese, under threat from Turkish invasion, also constructed a long line of lookout towers along the coast, atop which they placed their cannons in preparation for any attempted strike. When the need for military defence became less pressing, many castles were used as homes for the nobility or as shelters (a tradition also going back to the Crusades) by refugees and brigands. Some were converted into ready-made prisons or army installations. Because of their almost constant occupation, most of Puglia's castles are still largely intact and enhance both the landscape and the historical relevance of the area. Nonetheless, some have sadly fallen into ruin, such as those at Canosa di Puglia, or the evocative hilltop of Rocca di Garagnone.

Trani

Trani has never really looked back since the Middle Ages when it was a thriving and important sea-trading centre, and the many medieval churches and Baroque *palazzi* in the town still bear testament to its success through the centuries.

Castello

Although there's little here that is different to the many castles erected by Frederick II, the seafront location makes Trani's fortress more romantic than most, especially at sunset when it is bathed in a soft pink haze. Built in 1249, the castle witnessed the marriage of Frederick's son Manfred to Helena of Epirius a decade later. Its defensive structure made it an ideal setting for a prison in the 19th century, a role it fulfilled until 1975, but it has now been restored as a tourist sight.
Piazza Castello. Tel: (0883) 506603. Open: daily 8.30am–7.30pm. Admission charge.

Cattedrale di San Nicola Pellegrino

The most striking building in Trani, and in fact the whole coastal region of Puglia, is the seafront cathedral, dominating the harbour with its Romanesque rose-pink façade and elegant bell tower. The cathedral is best appreciated in the late afternoon when the sun has lost its heat haze and the beautiful building basks in a wonderful rose light, alongside the neighbouring castle. The vast bronze doors were the work of local 12th-century sculptor Barisano. Inside, the Romanesque detailing has been restored and there are beautiful marble columns in the crypt, but it is really the location that sets this cathedral apart from so many others. Adjacent to the cathedral is a museum that houses various sacred relics, sarcophagi and religious sculptures.
Piazza Duomo 8. Tel: (0883) 480557. Open: daily 9am–12.30pm, 3.30–6pm. Free admission. Museum: Open: Wed–Mon 10am–12.30pm.

Palazzo Caccetta

Of all of Trani's many *palazzi* this is the most famous and is now protected by the Italian government for its architectural splendour, in particular its Romanesque-Gothic façade. It was built in the mid-15th century for a local merchant.
Via Ognissanti 5. Tel: (0883) 494211. Open: Mon–Fri 9am–6pm. Free admission.

Bisceglie

Bisceglie offers attractions to suit all tastes – a well-preserved medieval centre, 15th-century city walls, an 'urban' beach and picturesque fishing harbour, and a rural idyll on its outskirts. There are also plenty of cultural places to visit for those who just can't resist a bit of sightseeing, including a Romanesque-Baroque cathedral dedicated to St Peter that has some Baroque embellishments (Piazza del Duomo), and an 11th-century Norman tower (Largo Castello).

Dolmen 'La Chianca'

About 5km (3 miles) outside of the town is the greatest archaeological find in the Bisceglie area, accessed via a lovely road lined with olive trees and vineyards. The ancient, prehistoric limestone tomb, dating from the Bronze Age, is one of the most significant in Europe because of its excellent state of preservation.

The seaside Cattedrale di San Nicola Pellegrino in Trani

Numerous funerary articles, jewellery and human remains were excavated here in the early 20th century.
Carrara Dolmen. Tel: (080) 3968084. Open: daily. Free admission.

Le Grotte di Santa Croce

Another of Bisceglie's most fascinating locations is this 100m (328ft) -long cave area discovered by a local archaeologist in 1937. Most of what was discovered here, including part of a thigh bone from Neanderthal man, is now on display in the town's archaeological museum. However, a visit to the grotto itself is recommended to take in its eerie atmosphere and understand just a little of the excitement that must have surrounded its discovery. Excavations are still ongoing – in 1997, a Neolithic basket was uncovered here.
Carrera Matina degli Staffi. Tel: (080) 3969233. Open: daily. Admission charge.

Cattedrale dell'Assunta, Ruvo di Puglia

Museo Civico Archeologico (Archaeological Museum)

Set within a former monastery, Bisceglie's archaeological museum is a gem of local finds, including Palaeolithic fossils, Roman relics such as ceramics and burial items and, most interesting of all in both a historical and local sense, remnants excavated from the Santa Croce grotto.
Via Giulio Frisari 5. Tel: (080) 3957576. Open: Mon–Fri 8.45am–1pm, Tue & Thur also 3.30–5.30pm. Free admission.

STRADA DELL'OLIO

The area around Canosa di Puglia, Andria, Castel del Monte and Corato is literally littered with olive oil producers, as is apparent from any drive in the region past the many groves of trees bursting with fruit. The Strada dell'Olio (street of oil) is a 150km (94-mile) designated tourist route that guides visitors to all the oil manufacturers (all producing the extra virgin variety) as well as pointing out the restaurants in the area that make the best use of the oil in their cuisine. For more information visit *www.stradaoliocasteldelmonte.it*

Ruvo di Puglia

Given its fertile surroundings, it's not surprising that Ruvo di Puglia has been a prosperous area since ancient times. Then, it was particularly known for its pottery work, contemporary samples of which are still for sale in the morning market in the street leading to the cathedral. Despite the unattractive, industrial approach to the town, Ruvo, as it is commonly known, is still renowned as a centre for local crafts.

Cattedrale dell'Assunta

This 13th-century cathedral combines both Romanesque and Gothic styles, peering down over a lovely medieval square. The main door is beautifully decorated with stone carvings of plants, animals and mythical beings, while above is a stunning Renaissance-style rose window. Other doorways are adorned with a masterful array of carvings that are among the richest collection in the area – human faces, the theatrical masks of Comedy and Tragedy, plant life and animals. Inside, too, the sculpture work is remarkable, including a central, intricately carved tabernacle, all of which lends the cathedral an elevated status in the region.
Largo Cattedrale. Tel: (080) 3611169. Open: 9am–8pm. Free admission.

Museo Archeologico Nazionale Jatta

Many of the priceless vases dating from the 6th and 7th centuries BC for which the town was best known were excavated in the 19th century and are now housed in this well-planned museum. Most of the distinctive black and red vessels depict scenes from the myths and legends of ancient Greece.
Piazza G Bovio 35. Tel: (080) 3612848. www.palazzojatta.org. Open: Mon–Wed, Fri, Sun 8.30am–1.30pm, Thur & Sat 8.30am–7.30pm. Free admission.

Molfetta

The main focus of Molfetta is its old town, with a lovely traditional fishing harbour and a seafront cathedral identified by its octagonal dome and towers and pale sandstone glowing in the sun. The most important sight, however, is less than 2km (1¼ miles) outside town. **Il Pulo** is a large, mysterious cave grotto area (170m/558ft long and 30m/98ft deep) where the most significant Neolithic remains in southern Italy were discovered at the turn of the 20th century. Most of the finds, including ceramic vases and blades made out

Molfetta harbour

of stone and bone, were invaluable for understanding the prehistoric way of life and are now on display in the archaeological museum in Bari (*see p43*).

Il Pulo. 2km (1¼ miles) from Molfetta. For opening times and details contact the local tourist office: Via Mattoli. Tel: (080) 3971001.

Bitonto

Bitonto owes much of its reputation to its production of high-standard olive oil, but it is also home to one of the finest Romanesque cathedrals in Puglia. Built in the 12th century, the triple façade dominates the landscape of the town, topped by a superb rose window. The highlight of the interior is the magnificently carved pulpit dedicated to Frederick II and his family.

Cortile Vescovado 5. Tel: (080) 3752100. Open: daily. Free admission.

Altamura

The area now occupied by the town of Altamura has been inhabited since prehistoric times, as witnessed by the discovery in a nearby cave of the *Uomo di Altamura* (Altamura Man), dating back some 400,000 years, as well as various megaliths. The town itself, however, owes its presence to Frederick II, who chose the site to create a *città libera* (free city). In this way, it became the most multicultural town in the area – Arabs, Jews and Greeks, as well as native Italians, thrived here in the Middle Ages, living in individual ghettoised areas that allowed them to trade and worship freely. Evidence of this can still be seen in the town; for example, the Greek Orthodox church of San Nicolò dates from the 13th century. Over the centuries, Altamura retained this reputation of diversity and independence, a price for which it paid heavily in 1799 when the town was ravaged by the forces of Cardinal Ruffo because it had supported the ideals of the French Revolution. Nevertheless, following the Unification of Italy the town was still seen as important enough to be the first seat of the Puglian government.

Cattedrale Santa Maria Assunta

Altamura's cathedral was built under the orders of Frederick II in the early 13th century, although it was largely reconstructed after an earthquake in 1316 destroyed much of the original. More dramatic alterations were made during the 16th century when the façade was reorientated to what was once the apse, and two bell towers were added, as were the lions which decorate the main door as a symbol of protection. The door is also notable for its depictions of scenes from the Life of Christ, including a *Last Supper* in which Jesus receives his kiss from Judas. Like many of the churches and cathedrals in the region, it received a number of Baroque additions in the 18th century, including elaborate spires. Inside, there is a wonderfully carved stone Nativity

scene and a beautiful marble altar depicting the Ascension.
Piazza Duomo. Tel: (080) 3117004. Open: daily. Free admission.

Museo Archeologico Statale

Those interested in learning more about the area's Neolithic and Bronze Age history should not miss the opportunity to visit the town's archaeological museum. Here, not only are excavated finds on display, but a full explanation of prehistoric Puglia is given.
Via Santeramo 88. Tel: (080) 3117679. Open: Mon–Sat 8.30am–7.30pm, Sun 8.30am–1.30pm. Free admission.

The Murgia

The Murgia (or Murghe) is the agricultural landscape found to the east and west of Altamura that is famous for its production of wine and olive oil. It has other regional specialities such as cherries, almonds, walnuts, cheese and *zampina* (sausages). There's an unmistakeable peasant feel to the region where many traditional farming methods are still employed, but there are also a few sights along the way such as the 12th-century castle in Gioia del Colle, another of Frederick II's edifices, and a beautiful cathedral in Sammichele.

Gravina in Puglia

Inhabited since prehistoric times and then an important agricultural area during Roman occupation, Gravina's present name originates from the 5th century AD when the inhabitants were forced to flee invading Barbarians and hide in a nearby grotto (*gravina*). It was subsequently ruled by the Normans and then the Orsini dynasty until the 19th century.

Duomo

Although Gravina's cathedral was originally built in the 11th century, it was almost entirely rebuilt in Gothic style following an earthquake in 1457. The rose window is one of the few features to survive from the original building. The interior is dominated by 14 columns decorated with capitals, a triumphal arch celebrating both the town and the Orsini family, and a 16th-century organ. In the sacristy the vestments of Pope Benedict XIII, a member of the Orsini family and referred to as the 'father of Gravina', are on display.
Piazza Duomo. Open: daily. Free admission.

Palazzo Ettore Pomarici Santomasi

Housed in a former palazzo of a local nobleman who left the residence to the town on his death in 1917, this museum is home to a collection of local treasures, including artworks from the 15th to the 17th centuries, historic costumes, a numismatic collection and, on the ground floor, a reconstruction of a crypt featuring 13th-century frescoes.
Via Museo 20. Tel: (080) 3251021. www.fondazionesantomasi.it.

Open: Tue–Sun 9am–1pm & 4–7pm.
Admission charge.

Purgatorio

The official name of this 17th-century church is Santa Maria del Suffragio, but its purpose as a family mausoleum for the Orsini family gives it the more commonly used nickname of Purgatorio (purgatory). Indeed, from the very moment you arrive here there can be no doubt of its purpose – the main door is decorated with a macabre depiction of skeletons. Inside, there are various Baroque works attributed to the craftsman Falcone, including giant statues and the Chapel of the Annunciation.
Piazza Notar Domenico. Open: daily.
Free admission.

San Michele delle Grotte

One of the town's most remarkable sights is this grotto-church built into the tufa rock and dating from around the 10th century AD. In the church, through a bright atrium, one can just about make out frescoes depicting Christ Pantocrator. Other features of the interior are the 14 sturdy pillars, statues of the three Archangels – Michael, Gabriel and Raphael – and, slightly less appealing, human remains of a few unfortunates who are supposed to have fallen foul of a Saracen raid in the 10th century.
1km (²/3 mile) outside town. Closed to the public.

Conversano

Although evidence exists of prehistoric inhabitants here, particularly by remains of ancient megaliths, Conversano today, set amid a landscape of olive and cherry trees, is a sleepy yet beautiful little town. There are rambling alleyways and a sun-baked piazza dominated by the Norman

The rolling hills of the Murgia

castle, with several Baroque embellishments. Also in the old town is the Romanesque cathedral.

Monopoli

The main sight in this walled, seafront town is its **cathedral**, originally dating from the 12th century but completely overhauled in Baroque style in the 18th century. Highlights of the marble- and stucco-filled interior include many artworks by leading Italian artists of the period including a *Last Supper* by Francesco de Mura. The flamboyant façade dominates the empty square, while to the right there is a wall filled with statues of biblical figures and saints. Adjacent to the cathedral is a **museum** housing relics from the 16th to the 18th centuries.
Largo Cattedrale. Tel: (080) 742253. Open: 8am–6pm. Free admission.

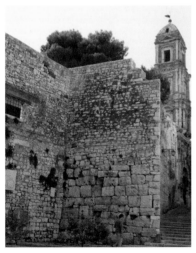

Monastero di San Benedetto in Conversano

Grotte di Castellana

Discovered in 1938, the grottoes of Castellana are an unmissable sight in any visit to Puglia. The vast complex of underground caves, 1.5km (1 mile) in length, offers breathtaking views of stalactites and stalagmites, as well as glistening crystallite within its many chambers. The caves can be visited as part of a guided tour – wear comfortable shoes.
2km (1¼ miles) from the town of Castellana Grotte. Guided tours: Apr–Sept hourly 9am–5pm; Oct–Mar hourly 9.30am–12.30pm. Admission charge.

Alberobello

Alberobello's claim to fame is its plethora of *trulli* houses (*see pp64–5*), but this has also in some way been its downfall – the town is now an overrun tourist centre, particularly along the Via Monte San Michele, where shop upon shop around eight streets in the area known as Aia Piccola sells model representations of the buildings fashioned with varying degrees of skill. Nevertheless, you'll see the most concentrated examples of *trulli* here (more than 1,000), many of which are still private homes, and learn about their history in a town that has dedicated itself to their preservation; UNESCO has even designated it a World Heritage Site. And, in a region that is largely bereft of places catering to tourists, it is quite refreshing to find somewhere that is so happy to have you visit.

For a more authentic experience of *trulli* in their natural surroundings, take a drive through the countryside around towns such as Cisternino (*see p71*), Ostuni (*see pp74–5*) and Martina Franca (*see pp108–10*).

Valle d'Itria & Locorotondo

One of the charms of Locorotondo is the approach to the town as you drive through the Valle d'Itria (Itria Valley) – a striking landscape of vineyards and traditional *trulli* in this highly agricultural area, and the sweet aroma of mint that grows by the roadside. The dry white *spumante* wine (DOC – *denominazione d'origine controllata*, meaning of the highest quality) is a speciality of the area – so much so that the town's nickname is *città del vino bianco* (city of white wine). The main feature of the beautiful town is the Baroque cathedral, with its domes seen far in the distance, but the whole town is a vision of blinding-white limestone houses and alleyways bedecked with geraniums and citrus plants. For a panoramic view of the valley from a higher vantage point, head to the public gardens at the top of the town.

The strange rooftop landscape of Alberobello

Trulli

One of the most magical aspects of the Puglia landscape, and one that has come to symbolise the region, is the quirky *trulli* (traditional) houses largely found in the Valle d'Itria district.

The history of these small limestone buildings, occasionally isolated but more usually clustered in small communities, is not entirely clear but most estimates date them to the Middle Ages. Their name derives from the Greek word *tholos*, which means 'dome' (although, rather charmingly,

A close-up of the *chiancarelle* roof stones

trullo in Italian means 'silly'). Originally, the houses were purely conical with the roof reaching to ground level, but in the 15th century they developed the squat whitewashed walls that can be seen today. The grey stones that make up the roofs are impermeable stones known as *chiancarelle*, and many feature symbols painted in limestone that were thought to ward off evil spirits. The houses were used primarily as peasant farmer accommodation, and the advantage of their construction and materials is that they remained cool in summer while retaining heat in winter. No one *trullo* is the same as another, as each one was hand-built without a specific plan. The entire building, including the roof, was constructed using drystone technique, that is, without the use of any kind of cement, which required a certain amount of building knowledge and skill. One of the reasons for this kind of construction has more than an air of myth about it – legend has it that when the tax on property became too high in the medieval period for the peasants, they simply pulled their houses down when the tax inspector called. With him safely sent on his way, they then rebuilt their homes.

The symbols painted on the roofs are to ward off evil spirits

As this practice caught on, however, it was also easy for the taxman to pull down homes himself if the debtors hadn't been quick enough to see him coming. By the 19th century, when these tax levies were abandoned, *trulli* could finally be built as more stable mortared constructions.

Internally, the single-storey houses are usually fairly bare – the rounded shapes can prevent excessive furnishing – with small windows and none of the rooms divided off by doors. Beneath the internal central dome is a platform that was traditionally used to store foodstuffs.

The best places to see *trulli* in their natural surroundings are in the countryside around Martina Franca, Locorotondo and Conversano, although the most famous gathering is in the town of Alberobello, which has now been designated a UNESCO World Heritage Site because of its more than 1,000 *trulli* houses (*see pp62–3*). Many of the *trulli*, which are repainted once a year to retain their glistening white exteriors, are still lived in by locals or are used as storage areas for their harvest. Many too have been converted into shops and restaurants, as well as accommodation either as part of a hotel or self-catering, which makes for a wonderfully unique stay. *Trulli* houses have also become increasingly popular as holiday homes for expats, particularly the British, a demand that sent their once trifling prices through the roof for some years.

Brindisi

No one with an interest in history or architecture should miss the opportunity to tour the province of Brindisi. From the fascinating ancient finds of Messapian cities such as Mesagne and Oria, through the incredible discovery of the skeleton of a pregnant Palaeolithic woman near Ostuni, to the Roman discoveries of Egnathia, the area offers one of the finest insights into the ancient world.

Architecturally, while the region is dominated by the legacy of Frederick II's irrepressible 13th-century castle-building, the Baroque period of the 18th century has left an even more beautiful mark, such as Francavilla Fontana. Add to this a rolling landscape of olive groves and vineyards, and the sun-baked *città bianche* (white towns) of Ostuni and Cisternino, their whitewashed buildings glimmering in the light, and the province has something to offer all holidaymakers.

Brindisi

Much like Bari (*see pp42–6*), the lifeblood of Brindisi is its port activities, particularly its passenger and cargo ferry services to Greece. Most people, therefore, visit the city as a

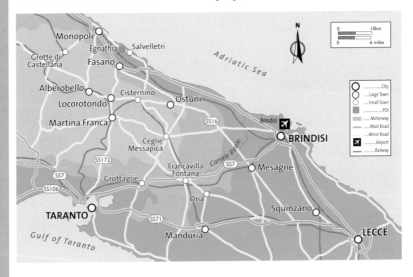

point of entry or departure, and this transient air has done nothing to enhance the landscape – it is, without doubt, Puglia's least attractive city. However, the port was the most significant southern Italian point in Roman times and the end stop of the renowned Via Appia. There are a number of ancient remnants of the Empire's glory days, and if you have a few hours to kill here, there are some sights worth taking the time to see.

Castello Svevo

It seems unlikely that Brindisi would be without one of Frederick II's beloved castles and it isn't, although little of the original, bar part of the walls and moat, is now visible. Frederick in fact built a total of four castles here, occupying a site between the city and the sea, which served not only as his residence but as administrative offices, a prison and an arsenal. More apparent are additions to the complex made by Charles I of Anjou at the end of the 13th century, Ferdinand I, King of Naples, two centuries later, and the Baroque embellishments of the 18th century.

The castle played an important defensive role against invading French in the mid-16th century, but this led to disaster for the city. During the campaign, the military leader of the castle mistook the enemy leader for a lesser soldier and in a bit of showmanship shot at him from the castle and killed him instantly. Rebellion ensued, with a brutal massacre of men, women and children.

During the 19th century, the castle served as a prison, but after Unification it became a base for the Italian Marines. It remains a naval base to this day, protected on its waterfront side by vast frigates. As a military stronghold, it is closed to the public, apart from organised tours.

Tel: (0831) 642111. Open: Mon–Fri for guided tours. Admission charge.

A panorama of Ostuni, one of the *città bianche*

Brindisi's Monument to the Italian Sailor

Monumento al Marinaio d'Italia (Monument to the Italian Sailor)

As an important naval base, Brindisi was chosen as the site for this national monument erected in 1933 in honour of all the Italian sailors who lost their lives in the fierce battles of World War I. The monument was funded in part by a series of classical concerts staged throughout the country. Following a national competition to decide on the design of the monument, the winners were architect Luigi Brunati and sculptor Amerigo Bartoli. They proposed the form of a giant rudder 53m (174ft) high, at the base of which is a crypt in the shape of a ship's hull, within which the names of the 6,000 sailors who perished in World War I and, even more tragically, more than 30,000 lost

REFUGEES

Puglia's coastal position between Europe and the Near East has always led it to be vulnerable to invaders and refugees. In earlier times, this could be a harmonious blend, as witnessed by the many Greek remnants in the area (*see opposite*), and has certainly assisted trade over the centuries.

In the 15th century, after an Ottoman invasion, many Albanians flocked here. Known as the Arbëreshe, there are still pockets of these communities, distinguished by their dialect and distinctive costumes. A peculiarity for Italy is that during much of the 20th century it witnessed mass emigration of its citizens, mainly to the US, so it was not as reluctant to accept foreign immigrants as many of its neighbours were. In fact, in 1986 a new law gave the new immigrants more rights and better chances of employment, partly in a bid to stop them hiding illegally.

Nevertheless, these lenient attitudes, combined with the increased struggles of the Balkans and the Middle East in the latter years of the 20th century and still ongoing, have proved an increasing problem for the government. Its port location means that Brindisi is a natural landing point for refugees and asylum-seekers from other countries – in particular the Roma (gypsies) of Kosovo and other regions, as well as displaced modern Albanians.

The proximity to North Africa also sees an influx of immigrants from those countries. Many live in unofficial camps in the area and, where once there was tolerance, there is now rising racial tension and potential danger. Not only does this affect Italy, and the south in particular, but the rest of the EU – once there, it's not difficult for the immigrants to move around a continent that has largely done away with border crossings. Since 2008, taking the lead from a number of other western European countries, Italy has embarked on a stronger crackdown on illegal immigrants and is considering reintroducing passport border checks. This will not halt the influx of people from countries such as Romania and Bulgaria, though, who are legally entitled to live in Italy as citizens of EU states.

sailors from World War II are inscribed on the walls.

Open: May–Sept Tue–Sun 9am–1pm & 3–8pm; Oct–Apr Tue–Sun 9am–1pm, 2–4.30pm. Admission charge.

Museo Archeologico Provinciale Francesco Ribrezzo

The strong links between ancient Greece and the Roman Empire found few more important meeting points than Brindisi, so it's not surprising that its archaeological museum is highly recommended. A wealth of statuary, ancient coins, ceramic remains and more fill its rooms. The undisputed highlight of the museum is the Punta del Serrone bronzes – a remarkable collection of 3rd-century BC bronzes that were discovered in the waters off Brindisi harbour in the early 1990s.

Piazza Duomo 7. Tel: (0831) 565501.

Open: Tue–Sat 9.30am–1.30pm, Tue 3.30–6.30pm. Admission charge.

Roman columns

The full extent of the Via Appia took some 150 years to complete in the 3rd and 2nd centuries BC under the auspices of various emperors, but in its final stages it covered a route from Rome all the way to Brindisi. A marble column and the remains of another (the original is now in Lecce) on the Lungomare Regina Margherita are thought to be parts of a monument erected to mark the end of the route.

However, there is some speculation about whether this was the true reason for the erection of columns here. Others believe the Romans cast them as a monument to the citizens of Brindisi for standing firm against Hannibal as well as donating both money and

Brindisi

Via Taranto is the main street in Brindisi

military support to the Roman cause. Whatever the reason, the columns, linked by a lantern, did serve a singular purpose as a navigational aid into the port, especially at night in a time before lighthouses, and as a symbol of the entrance to the city and the southern mainland. The existing column reaches a height of 18.7m (61ft) with a decorative capital of carved deities and acanthus leaves.

Egnathia

One of the most important archaeological sites to have been discovered in Puglia can be found at Egnathia (or Egnazia), which was once the location of a Greco-Roman town dating as far back as the 4th century BC. The excavated site is fascinating for its remains of ancient homes, a forum, a church and possibly an amphitheatre. The settlement was accessed by the Via

Greco-Roman ruins at Egnathia

Traiana, an offshoot of the Via Appia, which can still be made out. Perhaps most interesting are the stone tombs of the necropolis – some of the finest examples of their kind in Europe. To fully appreciate the history of the area, the value of its discovery and the ongoing works, don't miss the museum just outside the ancient walls that not only displays remarkable excavated pieces such as mosaics and vases, but explores the concept of archaeology in general.

Via degli Scavi 87. Tel: (080) 4829056. Open: Apr–Sept 8.30am–1.30pm, 2.30–7pm. Admission charge.

Salvelletri

This stretch of coastline, from Salvelletri down to Torre Canne, comprises what were once little more than simple fishing villages, and, indeed, daily fish markets (*except Monday*) are still a feature here. Today, however, attempts are being made to turn these villages into (largely Italian) tourist resorts, with hotel complexes, a golf course, nightclubs and bars as well as the more traditional fish restaurants. Visitors should not expect the sandy beaches more typical of Mediterranean holidays – the coastline here is rocky and craggy, and the waves on windy days can reach quite a height. For this reason, the area is popular with surfers and windsurfers. If you're touring the region and want a little rest and relaxation coast-side, the area makes for a nice day's break beside the sea.

A rare sandy beach near Salvelletri

Fasano

Another popular holiday resort, although a little inland from the coast, Fasano is dotted with a range of *masserie* (farmhouses), many of which have now been converted into atmospheric hotels and B&Bs. Most visitors are attracted by the Zoo-Safari, particularly families (*see p134*), but the town itself has a lovely laid-back but elegant feel, with whitewashed buildings and charming squares.

Museo dell'Olio d'Oliva (Olive Oil Museum)

This may seem like a bizarre theme for a museum, but more olive oil is produced here than in the rest of Italy and it is so intrinsic to the national cuisine that it's quite fascinating to discover the process from branch to bottle. Found in an ancient *masseria* (farmhouse), which is surrounded by around 60ha (148 acres) of olive groves, the museum explores the machinery and presses used in the production and explains the differences in quality

between virgin, extra virgin and plain old simple olive oil.

Contrada Sant'Angelo 5. Tel: (080) 4413471. Open: Fri–Sat 5.30–8pm. Free admission.

Cisternino

The olive theme continues in this lovely little town surrounded by vast swathes of olive trees, which make the town's nickname, *città per la pace* (city of peace), very apt. This is another of the region's *città bianche* (white towns), and within the pedestrianised historic centre, behind the Romanesque Chiesa di Madre, is a maze of whitewashed buildings bedecked with geraniums and potted ferns. The town is awash with simple, family-run *trattorie* (restaurants) and cafés, with names incorporating *zia* (aunt) and *nonna* (grandmother), enhancing the homely feel. Outside the pedestrianised area is the Belvedere with one of the best views of the Valle d'Itria (*see p63*) with its distinctive *trulli* domes. A lovely place to stroll around on a sunny day.

Olive oil

The production of olive oil is one of the oldest industries in Puglia and today accounts for more than 40 per cent of its entire agricultural income. With an estimated 50 million trees or more, Puglia is the main olive oil centre in Italy.

A large part of this success is due to the steady realisation around the world of the superior health qualities of olive oil compared to other oils, with the Mediterranean diet considered to be one of the most beneficial in terms of its effect on heart disease and obesity. This was understood even in ancient times.

Roman and Greek athletes were known to smear olive oil over their bodies to improve blood flow and enhance muscle development. The presence of Vitamin E and low levels of cholesterol in the oil benefits the body inside and out. Today, olive oil is used not just in cooking but in a wide range of cosmetics such as soap because the oil is proven to enhance skin quality and reduce the effects of ageing. No wonder olive oil is often referred to as 'liquid gold'.

Olive oil is produced in three general qualities which refer to the amount of acidity in the oil: 'clear'

A typical olive grove, thriving in dry ground

Pristine olives, ready for pulping

olive oil (*lampante*), virgin olive oil, and extra virgin olive oil. All the olive oil produced in Puglia is extra virgin, which means that there is less than 1 per cent of acidity per 100g (3½ ounces), and this is considered the most superior option. The oils are occasionally enhanced by the addition of local herbs.

The process of making olive oil is labour-intensive and, in its early stages, backbreaking work. First the trees must be harvested of the fruit and then, fairly swiftly so that the olives don't bruise, oxidise or spoil in any other way, they must be pulped into a paste. The paste is stirred vigorously before the final method of extraction is performed. Because of the methods required, it has been almost impossible to turn the olive oil industry into a high-tech affair. While modern machinery may now be used rather than traditional presses, the industry is still by and large a private one, with families of farmers tending to their own trees and producing their own oil as opposed to giant conglomerates.

Some of the best regions in Puglia for olive oil are the Salento region around Lecce (where the industry may have originated during the days of Magna Graecia), and Fasano and around Brindisi, which have been given a DOP (*denominazione d'origine protetta*) grading. The inland, flat plains are ideal ground for the production and harvesting of olive trees, which thrive in arid climates and continue to produce fruit for many years. To determine the quality of Puglia's extra virgin olive oil, the yellower the colour, the better it is.

The superior quality of Puglia's olive oil means that, as well as being used in traditional ways such as for grilling meats and dressing salads, it's common to see a bowl of oil on the table with a basket of local bread for dipping into the aromatic, flavoursome liquid as an *antipasto* (or 'starter').

Walk: Ostuni

You could be forgiven for thinking you've suddenly arrived on an island in the Cyclades when you reach Ostuni. Its whitewashed buildings and winding lanes are more than reminiscent of the villages to be found across the Adriatic. This is the most famous of the region's città bianche (white towns). The town is perched dramatically on a hilltop with wonderful views of the trulli-covered landscape and the olive groves surrounding it on the plains; from the latter, the town's skyline is dominated by the cathedral.

The *centro storico* (old town) of Ostuni is still surrounded by limestone walls used as a defence system over the centuries. If you're not staying in Ostuni, try to visit early morning or late afternoon. During the day it is a regular stop for tour buses and the town becomes crowded with American, German and British groups wandering single file through the narrow lanes.

This walk covers about 1km (²/₃ mile) and can be done in an hour, but bear in mind that the roads are steep and cobbled so sensible footwear is advised.

1 Piazza della Libertà

The heart of the town and home to the Municipio (Town Hall), a 20m (65ft) obelisk dedicated to the patron saint

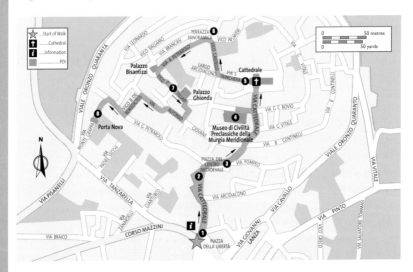

Sant'Oronzo, and a range of cafés shaded by cream parasols which makes a lovely refreshment spot.
From the piazza take the route up Via Cattedrale.

2 Via Cattedrale

The entrance to the *centro storico* (old town) is a hilly climb lined with shops selling local crafts such as sculpture and ceramics.
Continue up the street and turn right.

3 Piazza del Centro Medioevale

This pretty little square, as its name suggests, leads to the heart of the medieval centre, and is now occupied by a nice outdoor café and pizzeria.
Continue uphill up Via Cattedrale.

4 Museo di Civiltà Preclassiche della Murgia Meridionale (Museum of Preclassical Civilisation)

Set within a former 13th-century convent, this is one of the finest museums in the region for those interested in archaeology and prehistory. Various excavated finds from the Neolithic period to the Bronze Age are on display, with explanations about their past and their discovery. The most significant find here is without question the skeleton of the woman dubbed 'Delia' (*see p76*).
Convento della Monacelle, Via Cattedrale. Tel: (0831) 336383. Closed for renovations.
Continue up Via Cattedrale.

The white walls of Ostuni

5 Cattedrale

Although there has been a church on this site since the 13th century, much of the current edifice dates from the late 15th century when the church was remodelled and repaired following damage from an earthquake. The highlight of the façade is the rose window, which is decorated with astronomic and biblical themes, and has stone carvings depicting vines and wheatsheafs to illustrate the Eucharist of Christ.

The Latin-cross interior houses vast paintings showing scenes from the Life of Christ, various chapels dedicated to the patron saints of the town, and a sacristy containing priceless 16th-century artworks.

Via Cattedrale. From the cathedral, turn left down Via S Trinchera, and right down Vico Castello.

6 Terrazza Panoramica

This small square area offers wonderful views across the surrounding countryside of vineyards and valleys.

Turn left down Via A Petrarolo to the corner of Vico P Villari.

7 Vico P Villari

This small street is lined with 17th-century *palazzi* with Baroque portals, such as the Palazzo Ghionda and Palazzo Bisantizzi.

Narrow stone streets – great for exploring

Turn right, then left, then right, then right again into Via Alfonso Giovane, and continue straight until you turn left into Vico B de Benedictus. At the end of this street, turn right and then left into Via Monte Grappa.

8 Porta Nova

This is one of the gateways into the historic centre that was built during the Angevin period, and it gives a clear idea of how protected the inner alleyways of the medieval town were at the time.

Continue up Via Monte Grappa, turn left onto Via Tanzarella and return to Piazza della Libertà.

DELIA

Proof that the Puglia region was inhabited during the Neolithic period was incontrovertibly given when a 25,000-year-old skeleton of a woman was discovered in 1991 in a cave known as the Grotto of Santa Maria d'Agnano. The woman is thought to have been around 20 years of age at the time of her death, and one of the most remarkable and emotive factors of the find is that she was pregnant and the skeleton of her dead foetus was still recognisable in her womb. It is the first ever discovery of the remains of two prehistoric blood relatives in such immaculate condition. A member of a hunting tribe, Delia was discovered wearing a rabbit-skin cap, a shell bracelet and surrounded by rabbit skeletons embedded in the rock – part of the burial rites of the era because rabbits, for their skin and their meat, were of great importance to the hunters. After a complex operation to remove the skeletons without damaging the fragile bones, overseen by the Roman archaeologist who discovered her, Delia was laid to rest for all to see in the Museum of Preclassical Civilisation (*see p75*).

Ceglie Messapica

Although Ceglie has existed since ancient times as a Messapian city, most of the old town now dates from the medieval era. However, important excavations have uncovered Messapian burial sites from the 6th century BC onwards in grottoes around the modern town.

The medieval town, which was accessed via three gateways within the defensive walls, centres on the 14th-century castle. There are also several churches here that are notable for their 16th- to 18th-century art and architecture.

Pinacoteca Emilio Notte

Ceglie's most famous son was the Futurist painter Emilio Notte (1891–1982), whose works, donated by the artist himself, are now on display in this gallery housed in an 18th-century *palazzo*.
*Via P Chirulli 2. Tel: (0831) 387001.
Open: Mon–Sat 9am–noon, Tue 9am–noon, 3.30–7pm.
Free admission.*

Francavilla Fontana

Often referred to as the 'city of Emperors' because of the many beautiful *palazzi* built by noble families during the Baroque period, Francavilla Fontana deserves an hour or two of attention to take in these masterful buildings. The most famous is the **Palazzo Imperiali**, on Via Municipale, which combines the square

Chiesa Matrice, Francavilla Fontana

functionality of its original 15th-century castle origins (which is why it is sometimes referred to as Castello Imperiali) with flamboyant 18th-century additions such as the balcony and loggia. Today, its ground floor is home to the city council, but much of the rest of the building is undergoing renovation.

There are innumerable Baroque churches in the city that are worthy of note, but perhaps the most significant is **Chiesa Matrice**, dating from 1759. With its swirling, elegant tympanum, the wonderful symmetry of its portals and their stone carvings, and the charming fountain, it's a perfect example of the skill and imagination of the architects of the day. In a small chapel inside there is an icon of the Madonna della Fontana, the much-venerated patron saint of the town.

Oria

One of the most important Messapian towns in Puglia (*see p107*), Oria was also noted in medieval times for its thriving Jewish population, and there's still a historic Jewish quarter (*rione giudea*). Oria is now a popular tourist destination, not least for its wonderful views of two coastlines from its hilltop position – the Adriatic and the Gulf of

Oria's Castello Svevo

Taranto. The approach to the town, too, offers striking views of the castle and the dome of the cathedral.

Castello Svevo

Oria's wonderful castle, built between 1227 and 1233 to the orders of the indomitable Frederick II, still rises majestically from the landscape, between land and sea. Its stoic towers indicate that this was not a town to take potential invasion lying down.

The castle, although a national monument, is now privately owned by the Martini-Carissimo family. However, its luscious rooms and gardens are a popular venue for wedding receptions and other celebratory events, when visitors can wander the corridors that once played host to the nobility of days gone by.

Within the castle there is a small museum displaying remnants from the many epochs of Oria, from the Messapian era to the Romans and the Normans, as well as an art gallery of 16th-century paintings.
Via Castello. Tel: (0831) 845025.
www.castello-oria.it.
Closed for renovation.

Mesagne

Mesagne has much in common with other towns in the region: it was an important Messapian centre; its major sight is a medieval castle that was in the hands of both the Normans and the Saracens; it was much embellished during the Baroque period; and today it

ORIA'S PALIO

The tradition of the Italian *palio* (medieval joust) is generally more associated with northern Italy than the south, but every August Oria pulls out all the stops to re-create the atmosphere of the Middle Ages. On the first weekend of the month, the town's balconies are decorated with flags bearing the coats of arms of the four different *contrade* (districts) of the town (Castello, Giudea, Lama and San Basilio), all the way along to the Town Hall where the imperial throne is placed. Meanwhile, the horse riders (today selected from local athletes and volunteers), dressed in traditional garb and representing their particular district, prepare for the joust, accompanied by the enthusiastic cheers of the crowd. There can be only one winner, and the victorious district celebrates with wild excitement, dancing, acrobats and even falconers, conjuring up a strange world of medieval legend. At the end of the event, standard bearers, accompanied by drums and a trumpet salute, approach the young 'emperor' (another local volunteer) to commemorate the moment when he receives the hand of Jolanda in marriage from her father Giovanni di Brienne.

is surrounded by a lovely landscape of olive groves and vineyards. The highlight of the town, however, in a historic sense, is the excellent archaeological museum.

Museo Archeologico 'Ugo Granafei'

The importance of the city and the surrounding area to the Messapians (*see p107*) has resulted in highly successful excavations throughout the region, which have now all been brought together in this well-planned museum. Vases, ceramics, coins and mosaics from the Messapian and Roman eras are all on display, as well as silver and bronze items, intriguing terracotta animals that were thought to be used as children's toys, and fascinating finds from necropoli uncovered in the town. Some of the tombs have been fully reconstructed to illustrate the burial rites of the ancient peoples and their strong adherence to the death cult. The epigraphs uncovered provide great insights into the populations of these ancient times, some with names and dates still legible despite the passing of years.

Via Castello 5. Tel: (0831) 776065.
Open: Mon–Sat 9am–noon, 5–9pm.
Admission charge.

Hazy view from Oria's castle ramparts

Lecce and the Salentine Peninsula

Lecce is, undoubtedly, the jewel of Puglia – its compact, meandering Old Town is a paean to Baroque artistry, with every church façade virtually dripping with stone representations of foliage, animal life and religious imagery. Yet the region of Salento has more to offer. Otranto and Gallipoli are both charming seaports where the atmosphere of medieval trading still pervades the air.

History also plays a role just south of Lecce in the Uragano towns, where the Greeks brought not only themselves but their language and customs in days gone by. And, following the coast road to the very tip of the 'heel', past a range of mysterious and evocative sea caves, you can feel as if you're on the edge of the world as you look out from Santa Maria di Leuca across to the distant mountains of Albania.

Lecce

The beauty of Lecce, capital of the Salento region, often inspires gushing comparisons with better-known cities, most typically the 'Florence of the south'. While such terms are certainly complimentary, they don't offer any real sense of this unique little gem lighting up the 'heel' of the country. Lecce is its own city; its churches, *palazzi* and little alleyways are so lavishly adorned with a never-ending display of stone carvings in an area of little more than 3 sq km (1¼ sq miles)

that it would be hard to compare it to anywhere else in the world. It has attracted a great number of diverse religious orders over the centuries, including for a time a strong Jewish

population, hence the abundance of places of worship. For a short time in the 16th century, it was the capital of Puglia because of its abundance of administrative clerks. Nobles and aristocrats didn't hesitate to construct elegant residences and, of course, the town had the advantage of wonderfully talented architects and sculptors who created and mastered the Baroque style for which Lecce is now renowned (*see pp88–9*). All of this is found in the Old Town, surrounded by city walls begun in the 16th century; there is very little to interest the average visitor in the New Town apart from the train station.

Anfiteatro (Roman Amphitheatre)
Only about half of the original 2nd-century amphitheatre can be seen today, and this was excavated in the 1930s – the rest was covered over by subsequent constructions in the days before archaeological significance was appreciated. The amphitheatre was still used for entertainment purposes right up until 1982, but it is now protected by barriers and walls to preserve the fading stone.
Piazza Sant'Oronzo.

Castello
A Norman castle existed on this site for some centuries but, in the 16th century when Lecce was being consistently threatened by the Ottomans, Carlo V ordered that a more adequately defensive edifice be built here. The result was this sturdy trapezoidal

The Roman Amphitheatre, Lecce

fortress surrounded by solid battlements and an almost impenetrable moat. Much of the castle is now given over to tourist office facilities. Today, in front of the castle, there is a lovely garden promenade with an elaborate fountain where hawkers set up stalls to sell everything from North African carvings to plastic sunglasses.
Via XXV Luglio. Tel: (0832) 246517.
Open: daily 9.30am–6pm.
Free admission.

Mostra Permanente dell'Artigianato
Lecce is known for its crafts, most notably papier-mâché figurines, and this display is dedicated to explaining the skills and artistry that go into local products. As well as paper products,

there are details on the sculpting of local stone, iron-working, wood-carving, ceramics and weaving.
Via Rubichi 21. Tel: (0832) 246758.
Open: 9.30am–1pm & 4.30–8pm.
Admission charge.

Museo Provinciale 'Sigismondo Castromediano' (Provincial Museum)

Many of the finds that were discovered in the Roman Theatre and Amphitheatre, as well as ancient pieces unearthed around the rest of Puglia, are now on display in this excellent archaeological museum. Of particular importance are the black and red decorated vases that were typical of the region in ancient times, Roman statues, and artworks dating from the 15th to the 18th centuries.

Viale Gallipoli 28. Tel: (0832) 683503.
Open: daily 9am–1.30pm, Mon–Sat 2.30–7.30pm.

Piazza Sant'Oronzo

Away from the core of the Old Town, this large square is very much the heart of the city, surrounded by shops, restaurants, hotels and banks. Dedicated to the patron saint of the city, the piazza is dominated by a 35m (115ft) -high column, which once marked the end of the Via Appia in Brindisi (*see p69*), atop which sits a statue of Sant'Oronzo, who is said to have cleansed the region from a plague in the 17th century. Another dominant feature is the vast clock adorning the façade of the Banca d'Italia, decorated with the 12 signs of the zodiac.

The column in Piazza Sant'Oronzo, which once marked the end of the Via Appia in Brindisi

Historically, the highlight of the square is the view of the ancient Roman amphitheatre.

Porta Napoli
The Old Town of Lecce is entered via one of three gates, but the most impressive and largest is the 20m (65ft) -high triumphal arch of the Porta Napoli, constructed in the 16th century and decorated with the Habsburg coat of arms.
At the end of Via Principa di Savoia.

Porta Rudiae
At one time the main entrance to the city, before that honour was taken over by Porta Napoli, this gateway is an 18th-century reworking of a pre-existing gate, decorated with the city's three patron saints: Oronzo, Domenico and Irene.
At the end of Via Libertini.

Teatro Romano (Roman Theatre)
Like so many archaeological treasures, the remains of the Roman Theatre were uncovered by accident in 1929 when work commenced on the construction of a new house. Needless to say, the house was not built and excavations soon revealed the full orchestra area of the 2nd-century structure. The tiered seats can clearly be seen, remarkably intact, as can a long ditch running the length of the stage that would have been used to erect a curtain. The theatre is now entirely protected by railings and cannot be entered, but an

A fresco inside Lecce's castle

adjacent museum reveals both its history and its discovery.
Via degli Ammirati. Museum: Tel: (0832) 279196. Open: Mon–Sat 9.30am–1pm. Admission charge.

PAPIER MÂCHÉ

As well as the skills of its Baroque architects, Lecce is known for the craftspeople who constructed various forms out of papier mâché (*cartapesta*). Usually, these were made in the form of saints to decorate the city's many churches. A basic wire form is constructed and then adorned with a head, hands and feet made out of sculpted clay. Over the wire form, layer upon layer of paper dipped in glue is added and left to dry. Once the paper is firm, the sculpting of the model begins by burning and cutting away at the paper. Finally, the models are painted with a mixture of oil paints and distemper. Most of the churches in Lecce still feature at least one statue of this kind.

Walk: Baroque Lecce

If the beauty of Lecce can be attributed to any one aspect, it is to its Baroque architecture. While many other towns boast similar decorative features, none does so with the same exuberance. At every corner of the Old Town, you are met with examples – so much so that the style has a name all of its own: barocco Leccese *(Leccese Baroque, see pp88–9).*

The walk covers a distance of about 0.5km (¼ mile), but allow an hour for a leisurely pace.

Many artists were employed in the process of constructing and adorning the buildings, but the overriding influence came from the architect Giuseppe Zimbalo (1620–1710).

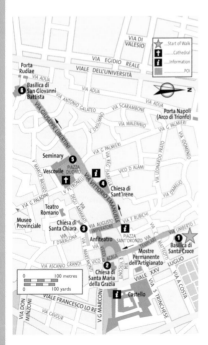

One of the main successes of the Leccese Baroque was that the local stone (*pietra leccese*) is of a pliable calcareous nature, allowing for ease of carving. As the Old Town is literally overrun with Baroque details, the suggested sights below are only the tip of the iceberg and include those that shouldn't be missed. Meanwhile, as you're wandering through the streets, don't forget to look out for the door knockers (*picchiotti*) on houses and buildings – even the most inconspicuous doorways often have intricate lions' heads, hands and faces marking the point of entry.

1 Basilica di Santa Croce

Probably the best-known Baroque church in the city, which is no mean feat when you consider the competition, the beauty of the basilica is hard to express in mere words.

Built on the site of a former temple in the 15th century, and lavishly

The Basilica di Santa Croce

decorated in the 16th and 17th centuries by a number of architects, but most notably Gabriele Riccardi, it takes some time to fully absorb the triumphant detailing of the façade. A variety of *putti* (stone figures) crams every centimetre of the space in the guise of monsters, lions, sea gods, cherubs and more, but the most striking feature is the rose window, the largest in Puglia. The lavishness continues inside with columns and marble altars all carved to within an inch of their lives, depicting saints and Apostles. Next to the church is a beautiful colonnaded former convent building that is now home to administrative offices.

Piazzetta Riccardi. Open: 8am–1pm & 5–9pm. Free admission.
Follow Via Umberto I then Via Templari along the side of Piazza Sant'Oronzo south and into Vico D Acala.

2 Chiesa di Santa Maria della Grazia

According to legend, this church was built because of a 15th-century fresco of the Virgin Mary here, where many miracles were said to have occurred. What we do know for certain today is that it was built over the top of the rest of the Roman Amphitheatre. The façade has a highly decorative tympanum above the main entrance and niched statues of saints.

A corner of Piazza Duomo

Via Alcala. Open: daily 9am–noon.
Turn right into Via Verdi, past the
amphitheatre, then left into Via Augusto
Imperatore.

3 Chiesa di Santa Chiara

With its highly decorative portal,
niches, column capitals and windows,
the façade displays all the florid
workmanship that gives Lecce its
reputation. Don't miss the papier
mâché ceiling inside.
Piazzetta Vittorio Emanuele II.
Open: 9–11am, 4–5pm.
Free admission.
Backtrack up Via Augusto Imperatore
and turn left into Via Vittorio Emanuele.

4 Chiesa di Sant'Irene

Dedicated to one of the three patron
saints of the city, this is one of the least
decorative façades among the Old Town
churches. This is made up for in the
interior, where the marble altars pull
out all the stops.
Via Vittorio Emanuele. Open: 9am–1pm
& 4.30–8pm. Free admission.
Continue along Via Vittorio Emanuele
until you see the entrance to Piazza
Duomo on your left.

5 Piazza Duomo

The courtyard that contains the
Duomo (cathedral), the Vescovile
(Bishop's Palace) and the Seminary is

undoubtedly the most impressive Baroque complex in Lecce. Try to visit at dusk when the setting sun bathes the pale golden stone in a magical light. The Duomo has been on this site since the 12th century but was lavishly rebuilt by Giuseppe Zimbalo in the 17th century, including the addition of the 72m (236ft) -high bell tower. Inside, there is a riot of marble and gold detailings. The bronze door, however, dates only from 2000, commissioned and erected to celebrate the millennium. The Bishop's Palace was also redesigned in the 17th century, with the addition of the clock atop the highly decorative loggia. The Seminary is distinguished by its beautiful loggia, windows and arches.

Duomo: Tel: (0832) 308557.
Open: 6.30am–noon & 5–7.30pm.
Free admission.
Exit the square and turn left into Via Giuseppe Libertini and continue to the end of the street.

6 Basilica di San Giovanni Battista

This sublime church, often called the Rosario, marked the culmination of Giuseppe Zimbalo's work in Lecce, and the great architect is buried in his final masterpiece. The façade is an explosion of flowers and saints, while inside the altars display Baroque flamboyance in all its glory.

Via Giuseppe Libertini. Open: 6.30am–noon & 5–7.30pm. Free admission.

The Vescovile (Bishop's Palace)

Barocco Leccese

The 17th and 18th centuries saw an explosion of the architectural style known as Baroque throughout the region, notably in towns such as Martina Franca (see pp108–9). Without doubt, the city of Lecce is the jewel in the crown of Puglia's Baroque period and, indeed, in all of Italy.

Historically, this trend for adorning churches and cathedrals with such flamboyant imagery can be seen as a celebration of the end of threatened

A Baroque balcony

Turkish invasion, finally put to rest in the Battle of Lepanto in 1571. With the Roman Catholic faith saved, it seemed appropriate to mark this victory in some significant way. In addition, Lecce had survived a plague in 1656, largely thanks to Bishop Otranto (now patron saint of the city), giving even further cause for jubilation. Combine this with the naturally soft calcareous local stone of Lecce, which was easy to work into the most intricate of shapes, and the unrivalled skills of the artists and sculptors that plied it into various forms, and the style known as barocco leccese (Lecce Baroque) was born. Among the greatest of the artists and sculptors were Giuseppe Zimbalo, also known as lo Zingarello (1620–1710), and Giuseppe Cino (1635–1722), both of whose visions define the city to this day.

That it all came together so cohesively in Lecce is in part due to the fact that there were so many churches, cathedrals and monasteries in the city by the mid-17th century because of an ambitious bishop. Coupled with this was a harsh taxation system that enriched the nobility, allowing them to spend vast

Extraordinarily intricate detail on the Basilica di Santa Croce

amounts of money adorning their homes with decoration as a sign of their prestige.

As well as the more obvious religious imagery of Christ, the Apostles and saints and angels, Lecce is awash with other altogether more whimsical and dramatic carvings. Corbels support balconies; fierce gargoyles look down from great heights; animals, both real and mythical, cling to façades and street corners, while human faces, often of citizens of the age, disguise the real architectural role of gutters collecting rainwater. Mother nature, and the abundance she brings, is also celebrated in the many examples of fruits, flowers and vines. The purpose of all of this is to engage the viewer, to demand their attention, so that they cannot fail to realise the importance of the church or the wealth of the resident.

It is not just sculptural skill that makes all of these additions so impressive; it's the theatricality and the humour with which they have been carved and placed, almost turning the city into a fantasy world.

Otranto

With a rich heritage of Greek, Roman and Byzantine occupation due to its strategic port-side location, Otranto came to the fore during the Middle Ages when it became a vital trading centre between the Adriatic nations. However, the town suffered a tragedy in 1480 when invading Turks massacred both the bishop and the majority of the citizens, 800 of whom were proclaimed martyrs because they refused to abandon their Christian faith – their bones are still venerated in a chapel in the town's cathedral. Today, the town is a popular tourist destination, with its wide beaches and wonderfully clear waters. In fact, the coastline here has been admired for centuries – it is even mentioned in Virgil's *Aeneid*.

A fresco in Otranto's cathedral

Castello Aragonese

The Aragonese took over Otranto following the Turkish tragedy and wasted little time in constructing buildings to suit their own needs, including this defensive castle. It was built on the site of an earlier 12th-century construction, but three towers were added to enhance its protective qualities. The castle today is best known as the subject of Horace Walpole's 1764 novel *The Castle of Otranto*, set during the time of Frederick II and considered to be the first Gothic novel.
Via Castello. Tel: (0836) 871308. Open: Tue–Sun 9am–1pm & 4–7pm. Admission charge.

Cattedrale dell'Annunziata

Otranto's cathedral has existed on this site since the latter half of the 12th century (the crypt existed a century before), but it was altered considerably after the Turkish onslaught and again in the 17th century when various Baroque embellishments were added, including a lovely rose window. Inside is a remarkable 12th-century mosaic floor depicting the Tree of Life.
Via Duomo. No telephone. Open: mid-Jul–mid-Sept 7am–noon & 3–8pm, mid-Sept–Jun 9am–noon, 3–5pm. Free admission.

Chiesetta di San Pietro

This 9th-century Greek-style church is known for its array of interior frescoes. On the altar they depict the Annunciation, the Apostles and the Resurrection; in the apse, the Last Supper; and in the nave, the Baptism of Christ.

Via San Pietro. Open: mid-Jul–mid-Sept 9.30am–noon & 4.30–8pm. Free admission.

Laghi Alimini (Alimini Lakes)

Now designated a national park area, these lakes offer a beautiful landscape of pine forests, hot springs and scrubland – a perfect day trip from Otranto for a picnic and a bit of inland bathing. Fishing is popular here too, with the lakes full of carp and mullet.

SS611, north of Otranto.

Santuario di Santa Maria dei Martiri

The Colle di Minerva (Minerva Hill) just south of the city is named after a supposed temple, dedicated to the goddess Minerva, which is thought to have existed here in prehistoric times. The sanctuary here today, however, is in honour of the 800 faithful Christians who were beheaded by the Turks in 1480. Five marble tablets record the names of the martyrs, while much of the rest of the interior is in Baroque style, using the famously malleable Lecce stone (*see pp88–9*).

Colle di Minerva. Open: mid-Jul– mid-Sept 9.30am–noon & 4.30–8pm. Free admission.

Torre dell'Orso

Just north of Otranto, this lovely stretch of sandy beach, backed by forests, has now become a popular tourist spot in summer with plenty of watersports opportunities.

Rocca Vecchia beach near Otranto

Greek heritage

The main Greek settlement of Puglia began in the 8th century AD during the time of the Byzantine Empire. The Iconoclastic Wars in Greece, whereby sacred icons were destroyed, forced thousands of faithful monks to flee the massacres taking place and to cross the Adriatic to southern Italy. They settled in what is now the Salento region, founded monasteries and created a small but thriving social and economic community. Their activities were not only confined to prayer; they were among the first in the region to begin the production of wine and olive oil, still a mainstay in Puglia.

In the following century, the Arabs plundered much of southern Italy, including Sicily and Calabria, again forcing faithful Christians to flee to Salento from these regions and from Crete, Cyprus and the Aegean. Among those fleeing were religious leaders and also functionaries, farmers, craftspeople and clerics; they discovered a landscape that had been largely uninhabited for centuries and were able to create successful villages. By the 10th century, there were some 40 villages between Otranto and Gallipoli that were almost exclusively Greek in every way – language, clothing, customs and religion.

Acropolis walls, Egnathia

Aerial view of Soleto

In the early 11th century, however, the Normans arrived in the region, bringing with them a feudal way of life and Catholicism. Suddenly, religious services were not conducted in Greek but in Latin. It was the beginning of the decline of the Greek communities who, in order to survive, abandoned their Orthodox faith for the new order, and their monasteries were gradually replaced by Franciscans and Dominicans. By the 17th century, only a small number of people who still spoke *griko* (the Greco-Salentine dialect) survived – around 13 villages. By the mid-20th century, this had fallen to just nine. Today, you are likely to hear the original dialect spoken only by the oldest of residents and, even then, only within the confines of their own homes.

In recent years, there has been a great resurgence of interest in the area's Greek heritage, and various cultural associations have been set up to preserve traditional songs and stories from centuries past, as well as encouraging studies about Greek-Salentine architecture, cuisine and customs.

There is now a proud and sustained rapport with Italy's neighbour across the Adriatic, unlike other minorities that often have troubled relations or misgivings about the 'motherland'. The Greek dialect of Salento is a minority language that is officially recognised by the Italian government. Moreover, as another symbol of the good relations between the two countries, a 4th-century marble pillar was donated by Athens to the village of Calimera in 1960, in honour of the local mayor at the time who worked hard to rediscover and reignite interest in the area's Greek history. The pillar is housed in a special pavilion that is inscribed with the motto '*Zeni esù en ise ettù 's ti Kalimera*' ('You are not a foreigner in Calimera').

Today, the Greek area is defined by the nine villages of Calimera, Castrignano dei Greci, Corigliano d'Otranto, Martano, Martignano, Melpignano, Soleto, Sternatia and Zollino.

Salentine Peninsula

From the 8th to the 11th centuries AD, much of the province of Salento was heavily influenced by the presence of Greek immigrants who had fled to the area due to religious persecution in their homeland, thus giving rise to the term 'Grecia-Salentina' (*see p93*). These small villages still bear witness to the time of Greek settlement in the region, with a local dialect (*griko*) still clearly showing Greek influences. Even the whitewashed houses with coloured shutters would not look out of place in the heart of the Cyclades. The Greek heyday ended with the invasion of the Normans, but numerous churches and monasteries still exist from that period and were also instrumental in forming a wine and olive oil industry still flourishing today. Signs to numerous towns still welcome visitors in both Italian and Greek.

Calimera

The very name of this town gives away its Greek heritage – Calimera (or Kalimera) means 'good morning' in Greek. Other Greek signs can be seen in the church of San Vito, which has a fertility stone (*pietra forata*) referring to a pagan rite that was also popular in western Greece. In the town, there are remains of cottages in a style typical of Greece because of the presence of their courtyards (*curti*). Elsewhere in Europe, peasant communities performed all their home-based work, such as the milling of grain, indoors; the Greeks, and therefore the Salento peasants, did these tasks outside in specially designed courtyard areas that contained wells and stables. Many of these cottages were later embellished during the Baroque era, making them unique

Looking across Martano on the Salentine Peninsula

examples of a style of house that proliferated in the Mediterranean.

Castrignano dei Greci

Just outside this village is a public park that is fascinating for its preservation of around 100 covered wells (*pozzelle*) that were once used to collect rainwater in order to irrigate the fields and provide drinking water for the inhabitants.

Corigliano d'Otranto

Corigliano was once home to a thriving school of Greek language and culture, and many of the manuscripts produced here are now preserved in museums and libraries around the country. The most memorable sight here is the 15th-century Castello di Monti with its four corner towers and balcony. It is currently undergoing restoration but visitors can still appreciate its imaginative architecture, including some lovely Baroque embellishments.

Martano

Like the rest of these towns, Martano has numerous churches and mansions attributed to its historic past, but its most famous sight is just outside town on a mountain between here and Caprarica. An ancient lookout tower, known as the Specchia dei Mori (Segla u Demoniu in the Greek-Italian dialect), according to legend, holds golden treasure that is in the hands of the devil. Regardless of this, the tower offers views across the Adriatic. Also here is one of the more important

menhirs in Puglia, San Totaro, reaching 4.7m (15^{1}/$_{2}$ft) in height, although today it is largely lost in the nondescript suburban street on which it sits.

Martignano

Many of the Urugano towns are home to 17th-century *palazzi* that belonged to the nobility, and the Palazzo Giuseppe Palmieri in Martignano is a particularly fine example. It is set, as was typical of the time, around a central courtyard. In the park next to the *palazzo*, there is a historic underground olive press. Part of the *palazzo* today is home to the tourist office. Also of note here is the Parco delle Pozzelle, where some ten ancient wells survive from the time when they once supplied the entire village with its water.

Melpignano

Probably the most important Baroque complex south of Lecce is the massive Augustinian monastery complex. Built in the 16th century in an attempt to convert the locals from Orthodox Greek to Catholicism, it still has a very strong northern European feel, rather than Greek. The façade was rebuilt in the 17th century according to plans drawn up by Giuseppe Zimbalo, that great architect of Lecce (*see pp88–9*). Sadly, the church suffered years of decay and has only recently been restored – little remains of the original apart from the choir stalls and a few altar sculptures.

Soleto

Soleto was a vibrant religious centre for the Greco-Italian inhabitants of the region right up until the 16th century, although most of the churches here now date from the Baroque period. The most striking sights are the Gothic tower attached to the church of Maria SS Assunta that was built for a member of the powerful Orsini dynasty, and the beautiful Byzantine frescoes in the Capella di Santo Stefano.

Sternatia

Sternatia's principal sight is the Chiesa Madre on Via Platea, begun in 1700 and most recognisable by the bell tower added almost a century later. The Palazzo Granafei is also worth a look – it is one of the most impressive noble houses of the Baroque period and is decorated with 18th-century frescoes.

Zollino

Various churches that celebrate the Baroque style of the region await the visitor to Zollino, but of most interest are the two menhirs that date from prehistoric times, and an ancient underground olive press.

Santa Cesarea Terme

As in much of the area, archaeological excavations have uncovered various signs of Palaeolithic life in this town, but its most significant assets are the thermal springs emerging from four caves, which are credited with having healing properties. The main spa, Villa Sticchi, is set in a Moorish-style building overlooking the sea, and has been attracting tourists for decades for its stress-relieving treatments, although its interior has clearly seen better days and visitors shouldn't expect the luxury of European counterparts. There's a beach in the town, but it's only accessible by boat or by descending a set of steep steps carved into the rock. *Terme di Santa Cesarea. Via Roma 40. Tel: (0836) 944070. www.termesantacesarea.it*

Grotte di Salento

The east-coast road of Salento (SS173) is littered with mysterious and evocative grottoes that have revealed numerous clues about life in this region in prehistoric times, and they have preserved a wonderful array of natural and human-made mysteries. Only the Grotta Zinzulusa is accessible by road; the others can be visited by taking a boat trip from either Otranto or Santa Maria di Leuca.

Grotta dei Cervi

Located at Porto Badisco, this cave contains one of the most spectacular examples of cave painting in southern Europe, including depictions of deer hunts from which the cave gets its name, and other aspects of daily life in the prehistoric era.

Grotta Romanelli

Cave paintings adorn this enclave – an image of an ox being speared is thought to be more than 11,000 years old – but more significant, perhaps, are the Palaeolithic fossils of animals that once frequented the region, including, amazingly, elephants.

Grotte Tre Porte, dell'Elefante and dei Giganti

Fossils of elephants and other animals more readily associated with Africa have been found here.

Grotta Zinzulusa

The most accessible cave in the region, near the town of Castro and accessed by purpose-built steps, is known for its stalagmites and stalactites. The spectacular entrance leads to the Corridoio delle Meraviglie (Corridor of Marvels), where the best rock formations can be seen, followed by a crypt area glistening with crystal formations. An outdoor swimming pool is another attraction here.
Tel: (0836) 943812.

Santa Maria di Leuca

Often referred to as *Finibus terrae* (the end of the earth), the southernmost tip of Puglia and Italy's 'heel' is an evocative place where the Adriatic and the Ionian seas meet, and it is only 800km (500 miles) from northern Africa. The town is dominated by the 60m (197ft)-high cliff topped by a lighthouse that can be seen from 30km (18 miles) away, and from which the views out across the sea can be breathtaking.

The town's most famous sight is its hilltop sanctuary. Supposedly built on top of a pagan temple to Minerva, it has long been a popular pilgrimage site. Other attractions of the town are the grand mansions built in the 18th and 19th centuries by wealthy nobility in a variety of exotic architectural styles, from Gothic through Moorish to mock-Chinese.

Along the beach, two small stone huts known as *bagnarole* were originally built so that women could sunbathe away from the prying eyes of men, but today they are used for storage.

Gallipoli

Like the majority of the towns in the region, Gallipoli has had a mixed bag of rulers in its history. The Greeks (the name Gallipoli comes from the Greek

Villa Sticchi in Santa Cesarea Terme

Kale polis, which means 'beautiful city'), the Romans, the Normans, the Angevins and the Aragonese have all vied for control of this important port. Unsurprisingly, they have all left their mark on the landscape. Today, however, Gallipoli's fishing harbour, which has long been so important to its economy, is a favourite tourist spot with its seafront restaurants and atmosphere. Unlike most towns of the region, Gallipoli's New Town is also a vibrant centre of restaurants and cafés rather than the more usual bleak municipal façades.

Castello

Linking the Old and the New towns via a bridge, the seafront castle was an important defence structure against invaders wanting to take over this prosperous port. It was built by the Angevins in the 13th century, although, like much in the region, it was considerably altered in the 17th century. Today, it's an evocative symbol

Fishermen, Gallipoli

of days gone by amid modern catamarans and other sailing vessels. The castle also features an open-air theatre venue, currently undergoing restoration.
Between the Lungomare and Corso Roma. Closed for renovation.

Cattedrale di Sant'Agata

This beautiful Baroque cathedral right in the centre of the Old Town was built in the 17th century on the site of a former medieval church. The façade is a wonderful example of the sculptural skills of the time, carved in Lecce stone (*see p88*). Sadly, the intricacy of the façade is now somewhat lost amid the shops and cafés that crowd around it. Inside, there are reliquaries of various saints, although the 'breast' of Saint Agatha that once resided here is now in a church in Galatina.
Via Duomo. Tel: (0833) 261987. Open: 7am–noon & 4–9pm. Free admission.

Fish market

In the shadow of the castle, Gallipoli's lively fish market echoes with the cries of traders selling the day's catch. Within each stall there are likely to be piles of vast ranges of fish from tuna, monkfish and swordfish to squid, mussels and octopuses. Other sea-themed goods are also on sale, including ceramics decorated with marine scenes, and shells and sponges. And, of course, there are the obligatory bowls of olives.
Largo Dogana. Open: Tue–Sat 8am–1pm. Free admission.

Gallipoli's castle and harbour

Fontana Greca

One of the oldest fountains in Italy, near the bridge that connects the Old and New towns, Fontana Greca possibly gets its name from the Greeks who once inhabited the area, although it more likely dates from the Renaissance era when interest in Ancient Greece was at its zenith. It is decorated with bas-reliefs of scenes from Greek mythology.

Museo Civico 'E Barba'

Gallipoli's Greek and Messapian heritage is uncovered here with a display of excavated vases and coins. There's also an interesting section devoted to the natural landscape of the area, both flora and fauna.

Via A de Pace 108. Tel: (0883) 264224. Open: Mon–Fri 9am–1pm & 2–4pm, Sat 9am–1pm. Free admission.

Palazzi

One of the most attractive aspects of wandering around Gallipoli's Old Town is its abundance of 17th-century *palazzi*, built for the wealthy who had made their money from the lucrative export of olive oil. The decorative Baroque carvings adorning the façades and the intricate wrought-iron balconies were all embellishments designed to display the owners' wealth and prestige. Among the best surviving today are the Palazzo Tafuri and the Palazzo Venneri.

Galatina

Much like Gallipoli and the other towns in the area, Galatina has many remnants of its former Greek occupation, along with a beautiful late Romanesque church. It is also an important wine-producing and tobacco-farming area.

Basilica di Santa Caterina d'Alessandria

This medieval Romanesque church was built when the town was under the rule of the Orsini dynasty, and little expense was spared in its design. The façade is adorned with statues of Christ and his 12 Apostles, as well as a lovely rose window. The interior has an array of columns, burial tombs of the family, and frescoes depicting biblical scenes. *Piazza Orsini. Tel: (0836) 568494. Open: 8.30am–12.30pm & 4.30–7pm. Free admission.*

Museo Civico d'Arte 'Pietro Cavoti'

This small museum is dedicated to the works of two local artists, the 19th-century sculptor Pietro Cavoti and the 20th-century Gaetano Martinez.

Piazza D Alighieri 51. Tel: (0836) 561568. Open: Tue, Thur & Sat 9.30am–1pm & 4.30–8pm, Wed, Fri & Sun 9.30am–1pm. Free admission.

Nardò

Nardò is not often frequented by tourists, and at first glance it's easy to see why, with its largely unprepossessing appearance. However, it does boast some historic monuments, such as the Baroque-style Piazza Antonio Salandra dominated by the Guglia dell'Immacolata, and the elegant Piazza Mercato shading a range of shops beneath its lovely porticoes. Other sights include the

The castle in Copertino

one-time castle, part medieval, part Baroque, and home to the botanical gardens, which now houses the town's administration offices, and the 11th-century cathedral.

Copertino

Much of the landscape of Copertino's Old Town has changed little since the 16th century. Its most famous attraction is the dominating Renaissance castle, completed in 1540 on the site of a former Norman fortress. Like others in the area, the castle was built as a defensive measure. The interior includes original living areas, frescoes, and some remnants of the Norman past. The town is also famous for the story of San Giuseppe, so much so that its nickname is the *città di Santo involi* (city of the flying saint). A church dedicated to the saint, the **Chiesa San Giuseppe da Copertino**, explains his remarkable life. *Via Castello. Tel: (0832) 930722. Open: 8.30am–1.30pm. Admission charge.*

THE FLYING MONK OF COPERTINO

The man who would come to be known as San Giuseppe (St Joseph) was born in Copertino in 1603 and began having visions by the age of 8. At the age of 17, he was keen to follow in the footsteps of two uncles and join the Franciscan Order. However, never having excelled in academic studies, he was initially refused entry by the monks but was eventually accepted as a servant within the monastery. Desperate to prove his humility and devotion, if not intelligence, Giuseppe finally passed the exam to enter the order in 1627 but only because the examiner fortuitously asked him the one question that he had managed to memorise. A year later, Giuseppe was promoted to the priesthood, but only because of the achievements of his fellow examinees rather than through his own abilities.

What eventually marked this poor contender out was a follow-on from his childhood visions – he began to experience periods of ecstasy during which his body levitated into the air, and he was purportedly able to speak to God. Alarmed by these events, Giuseppe's fellow brothers attempted to halt the trance-like occurrences, even poking him with pins and burning him with hot coals, but to no avail. At times, Giuseppe was seen to 'fly' mid-air towards the church altar, earning him the nickname the 'flying monk'.

Pope Urban VIII was present at one of Giuseppe's more than 70 levitations and attested to what he had seen. Gradually people began to come to the monk to ask for help and healing, and he is said to have performed numerous miracles – restoring sight to the blind and curing the incurable, as well as being able to predict events such as the death of popes. Inevitably, there were some doubting Thomases who thought that the whole business was a con, and Giuseppe was eventually called to a tribunal in Naples. During his inquisition, he levitated again, but regardless of this he was held under suspicion and sent from one isolated monastery to another in an attempt to hush the phenomenon. He lived under a strict regime and was forbidden to write or receive letters from his many devotees – an imprisoned way of life that continued until 1657 when Giuseppe was finally reinstated with fellow monks in a monastery near Loreto, that most holy of Italian sites. He died in 1663 and is buried in the basilica named after him in the town of Osima, his last place of worship. San Giuseppe was canonised in 1767 by Pope Clemente XIII, and he is now, unsurprisingly, the patron saint of pilots.

Taranto

The smallest of Puglia's regions is dominated by the industrial port town of Taranto, which is not only an important economic centre in the production of steel but is also the main naval base of southern Italy. However, the region also boasts some beautiful landscapes for nature lovers, in particular the crags and cliffs of the rupestrian (rocky) towns. And Martina Franca is a gem of a Baroque town, on a smaller and less overwhelming scale than Lecce.

Taranto

The 'city of two seas', Taranto has been an important settlement in southern Italy since time immemorial. One-time capital of Magna Grecia, the Romans and Byzantines saw the potential of its harbour location, a feature that has continued to advance the city's success. These days, however, Taranto gets something of a bad press, which isn't entirely justified. True, industry, and in particular steel production, is the backbone of Taranto's modern economy and does blight the

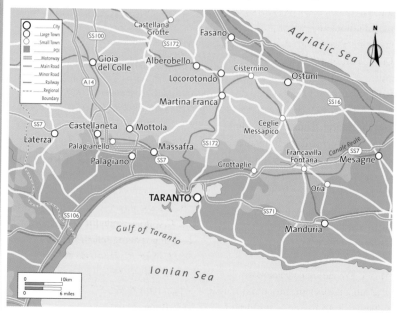

Taranto's castle is now used as a base for the Italian Navy

landscape, and the city is still an important naval base, but there's something quite romantic about seeing Italian sailors in their crisp white uniforms roaming around town. Unlike almost all the other Puglian cities, where the attractions still lie within the historic centres, Taranto has a New Town that is an elegant and sophisticated area of 18th- and 19th-century buildings, fountains and pedestrianised promenades. Its Old Town, in contrast, is depressingly slum-like in its appearance and attitudes, despite the many historical treasures that lie within its murky alleyways.

Museo Archeologico Nazionale

The most important museum in Puglia is Taranto's Archaeological Museum.

Here, excavated finds from around the region as well as from the city itself, largely uncovered during road building in the middle of the 20th century, are displayed. Among the exhibits are ancient vases, bottles, cups and other ceramics from Roman times and earlier. The most famous collection is the Salon of Gold, which displays elaborate jewellery and other adornments dating from the days of Magna Grecia (4th to 1st centuries BC). The museum has been undergoing extensive renovation since 1998 but visitors are able to view collections on the first floor while the rest of the building is being refurbished.

Via Cavour 10. Tel: (099) 453211.
www.museotaranto.org.
Open: daily 8.30am–7.30pm.
Admission charge.

Walk: Taranto Old Town

Taranto's centro storico (old town), accessed across the Ponte Girevole from the New Town, is dominated by its castle which is still home to the Italian Navy. Surrounded by two stretches of water, the Mar Grande and the Mar Piccolo, the area's outskirts make for a pleasant waterside stroll. However, within the Old Town is a warren of alleyways and cobbled lanes that could ambitiously be called romantic, but in truth is rundown and, at times, can be menacing.

The area is on the cusp of undergoing regeneration which should eventually lend it a more evocative feel, but at present the work has left a number of abandoned buildings supported by scaffolding that add to the impoverished air. When walking in the area, stick to the main sights, leave valuables at home or out of sight, and avoid going off the beaten track, particularly at night.

The round trip covers an area of approximately 2km (1¼ miles) and can be walked in a little under 2 hours. Starting in the New Town, cross the Ponte Girevole and walk through Piazza Castello to the Piazza Municipio.

1 Tempio Dorico

The ruins of these two Doric columns are all that is left of what was once

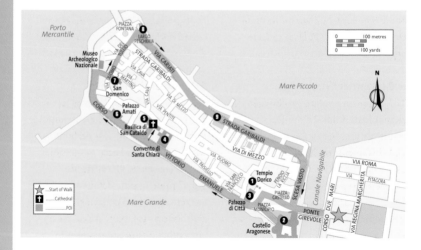

one of the most significant temples in Magna Grecia, dedicated to the god Poseidon. Kilns and cisterns in the area were also excavated in the 1920s.

Piazza Municipio.
Cross the square to the castle entrance.

2 Castello Aragonese

There is no clearer proof of Taranto's trading significance than the dominating façade of its castle. Built in the 15th century as a necessary defence measure against invading Turks, it is notable for its four sturdy cylindrical towers from which cannons could be fired through designated holes. When defence was no longer such an issue, the building was turned into a prison in the 18th century but was donated as a base for the Italian Navy in 1887.

Piazza Municipio. Tel: (099) 7753438.
Open for guided tours: Mon–Fri
9.30–11.30am, 2.30–5.30pm,
Sat & Sun 9.30–11.30am. Admission
charge. Walk to the Palazzo di Città
opposite the castle.

3 Palazzo di Città

This governor's palace was built in the second half of the 18th century and features a number of Baroque embellishments on its façade, typical of the day.

Closed to the public.
Facing the palazzo, *with the water on*
your left, walk down the waterfront on
the Corso Vittorio Emanuele.

The two Doric columns of Tempio Dorico

4 Convento di Santa Chiara

This cloistered convent is distinguished by its polychrome mosaic tiles in the chapel and its arched porticoes.

Turn right up Vico Santa Chiara.

5 Basilica di San Cataldo

The façade of this 17th-century cathedral is adorned with Baroque details that were influenced by the work going on in Lecce in the same period (*see pp88–9*). Inside are polychrome marble details and eight attractively carved columns. The archbishop's palace next door is currently undergoing renovation.

Taranto fishing boats

Open: 8am–noon & 4.30–7.30pm.
Free admission.
Return to Corso Vittorio Emanuele and
turn right.

6 Palazzo Amati

This 18th-century *palazzo* is now home
to a school, but its façade, with its
elegant proportions and wrought-iron
balconies looking out over the sea, can
still be admired.
Continue along Corso Vittorio
Emanuele as the road bends around
the harbour and turn right up Vico
Pietro Imperiale.

7 San Domenico

A highlight of this medieval church
is the lovely rose window, although
the entrance stairs are pure Baroque
in style, having been added in the
18th century. Beneath the adjoining
convent, remnants of ancient walls have
been unearthed.

Walk north along Via Duomo and then
Via del Tullio, past the Piazza Fontana to
Largo Pescheria.

8 Largo Pescheria

The traditional fish market area is still a
bustling part of the Old Town, a meeting
place for locals among the din of
motorcycle engines. The adjacent
fountain in the square, together with a
few surrounding hotels, has sadly seen
better days.
Walk east up Via Cariati along the
harbour front to Strada Garibaldi.

9 Strada Garibaldi

This promenade is the mooring point
for local fishing boats as well as
pleasure craft, and there are usually
local boys kicking a football about on
the wide pedestrianised strip.
Continue up Strada Garibaldi, turn
right into Scesa Vasto and return to
Ponte Girevole.

Manduria

Manduria's history stretches back to the Messapian era, and one of the most important Messapian remains is to be found on its outskirts. Although today it's a slightly staid, workaday town, it's largely known now as an important oil and wine producer, and the many wine cellars on the run into town are a good place to stock up on cases of Puglian *vino* (wine). The heart of the town is Piazza Garibaldi, dominated by the 18th-century Palazzo Imperiali (now a bank), with its intricate wrought-iron balcony along the otherwise largely unadorned façade. Several other Baroque *palazzi* can also be seen in the town, as well as a lovely Romanesque cathedral with a striking rose window. A collection of Messapian ceramics can be seen in Manduria's library.

CERAMICS

Many areas of Puglia are renowned for their production of ceramics, but the heartland, blessed by an abundance of clay, must be the town of Grottaglie, where you can't fail to notice row upon row of vases and pots drying in the sun. The same skills and craftsmanship that have been in existence here since the Middle Ages are lovingly and proudly preserved, with artists reproducing the same colours and shapes that have been made for centuries in this region. One of the reasons that the craft has survived so well is thanks to the opening of an art school in the town in the late 19th century. Even today, art students flock here to learn the techniques, and artisans' shops are still booming businesses.

MESSAPIANS

The Messapians came to the southern region of Puglia from Greece and Illyria (modern-day Albania) around the 5th century BC and established independent city-states in their new territory. Their livelihood was working the land and breeding horses as well as trading with Greece across the Adriatic. They lived contentedly alongside the native Puglian residents, but were either killed or carried into slavery when the Romans conquered the south, largely because they had supported Hannibal and his Carthaginian troops.

Parco Archeologico delle Mura Messapiche

Just on the edge of Manduria is a collection of important archaeological finds, now protected by gates within the *zona archeologico* (archaeological zone). The Fonte di Plinio (Pliny's font) is an underground grotto fountain, so-named because the great Roman historian Pliny mentioned it in his writings. The fountain can be accessed by stairs carved into the rock, or you can peer down through the protective wall to the bottom. Beyond this are the Messapian walls dating from around the 5th to the 3rd centuries BC. The walls can be seen either as part of a tour or from a viewing platform, which gives a better impression of the scale of the find.

Zona Archeologico. Open: Tue–Sun 9.30am–12.30pm, 2.30–7pm.
Guided tours on request.
Admission charge.

Walk: Martina Franca

Perhaps second only to Lecce (see pp80–89), Martina Franca is a must-see town for its beautiful Baroque architecture, atmospheric alleyways and stunning palazzi. The town largely grew up in the 14th century with tax exemptions from Philip of Anjou, but its legacy was assured by increased wealth in the 18th century.

The walk covers approximately 0.5km (¼ mile) and should take between half an hour and an hour.

The town is also known as something of a gastronomic gem, incorporating the produce from its surrounding landscape to create wonderful cheeses, pasta, cold meats (*capocollo* is the speciality) and a more than palatable dry white wine. The walk around the heart of the *centro storico* (historic centre) is, however, only an introduction to the town –

meandering down little alleyways and lanes will bring you face to face with many more delights.

Start at the Piazza XX Settembre.

1 Piazza XX Settembre

The town's main square, just outside the *centro storico*, and once the centre of trade and markets, is still a meeting

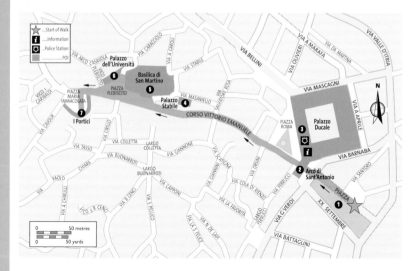

place for locals, with cafés and bars lining its pedestrianised centre.
Walk to the northern end of the square and the corner of Via G Verdi.

2 Arco di Sant'Antonio

The entrance into the *centro storico* is this impressive Baroque triumphal arch typical of the period. Once known as Porta di Santo Stefano, it is decorated with a figure of the saint.
Walk through the arch to Piazza Roma.

3 Palazzo Ducale (Ducal Palace)

Built on the site of the 14th-century Orsini castle, this 17th-century building, designed by Carducci, is one of the loveliest in town, notable for its wrought-iron balcony. The building was built for one of the Caracciono dukes, Petracone V, in a gesture of great self-importance, and inside there are three halls adorned with paintings by Domenico Carella depicting the ducal family in scenes representing Greek mythology.
Part of the building is now home to the Town Hall. In front of the *palazzo* is the lovely Dolphins Fountain, flanked by palm trees.
Piazza Roma. Tel: (080) 4836111. Open: Mon–Fri 9am–1pm & 4–6pm. Free admission.
Leave Piazza Roma by the southwest exit and walk right along Corso Vittorio Emanuele. Just before reaching Piazza Plebiscito, look to your right.

Arco di Sant'Antonio in Martina Franca's *centro storico*

4 Palazzo Stabile

Mussolini's minions made their home here during the Fascist era, but today it can be admired for its unusual terracotta-coloured façade, which includes arched windows.
Via Masaniello. Closed to the public. Continue along to Piazza Plebiscito.

5 Basilica di San Martino

A stunning example of Baroque detailing can be seen on the façade of this collegiate church, with carved depictions of the saints Peter, Paul and the namesake, Martin. A dazzling array of stained-glass windows and marble detailing can be seen in the interior, the most colourful of which decorates the altar. Also within the church is a depiction of the *Last Supper* by Domenico Carella.

Via Massarietto 1. Tel: (080) 4306536.
www.basilicasanmartino.it.
Open: daily 7.30am–12.30pm &
4.30–11pm. Free admission.
With your back to the church, cross the square to your right.

6 Palazzo dell'Università (University Palace)

This 15th-century building, which used to house the local parliament, is adorned with flamboyant stone carvings over its windows and portal, and is flanked by the considerably more Baroque Municipal Clock Tower.

Piazza Plebiscito.
Cross the square again, this time to your left, to Piazza Maria Immacolata.

7 I Portici

These lovely Baroque porticoes are now home to two restaurants (*see p157*), but their elegance has not been lost in the conversion.

A view of the Basilica di San Martino

Grottaglie

Grottaglie is best known for its highly skilled production of ceramics and the *quartiere delle ceramiche* (ceramics quarter) along Via E Crispi, just outside the entrance to the *centro storico*. The castle area is still lined with potters' workshops and stores selling the famous pots, barrels and crockery. At Christmas and during the height of the summer season, there's a large market to celebrate the local skills. Also in the town is the 12th-century Chiesa Madre.

The Rupestrian towns

This region of Puglia is unique for its canyons and ravines (*gravine*),

The castle in Grottaglie

reminiscent of America's southwest. Not only does the countryside make for ideal trekking and hiking, it has necessitated several dramatic towns cut into the cliffs ('*rupestrian*' literally means 'rocky').

Castellaneta

You can't fail to miss the fact that this small town was the birthplace of the Hollywood idol Rudolph Valentino (*see p112*) – it seems as if every bar and café is named after him, and there's a bizarre statue to the man dressed as a sheik in psychedelic blue at the entrance to the town and a large portrait in a tiny street within the historic centre. A museum dedicated to the actor features photographs, scripts, scenes from his films, including part of the set from his most famous film *The Son of the Sheik*,

Valentino mural, Castellaneta

Massafra's castle

as well as the remarkable footage of his funeral. That aside, the town is perched dramatically on the edge of a ravine and is home to an impressive cathedral and many other churches such as the Romanesque-style Chiesa Santa Maria.
Museo Rodolfo Valentino: Via Municipio 19. Tel: (099) 8492348. Open: daily 10am–1pm, 5–7pm. Free admission.

Laterza

On the far reaches of Taranto province, Laterza is best known for its cave churches dating back several thousand years that are adorned with rock art. Most are only accessible by taking an organised tour, but the entire region is a haven for hikers.
Tel: (099) 8296007 for tour information.

Massafra

First documented in AD 970, Massafra sits on a ravine that cuts it in two; the New Town and the Old Town are linked

RUDOLPH VALENTINO

Castellaneta's most famous son was the Hollywood heart-throb of the silent movies era, Rudolph Valentino (1895–1926). A fairly idle youth, Valentino emigrated to America in 1913 and earned his living initially as a dance teacher, before moving to Hollywood where he played bit parts in a number of silent movies. His big break came in 1921 when he got the part that defined his career – the lead role of *The Sheik* – and a few years later the sequel, *The Son of the Sheik*. He became known as the 'great lover' of his generation, swooned over and adored by millions of movie-going women. At the height of his fame, Valentino returned briefly to Italy and his home town. His tragically early death from peritonitis at the age of 31 witnessed unprecedented mourning on the streets of New York, which risked turning into a riot until police were called in to calm the hysterical female population. Despite his iconic status among women, rumours have long persisted that Valentino was in fact gay, partly due to his feminine appearance and partly due to two marriages to lesbians, but this has never been proved. He remains, to this day, the symbol of male ardour.

by two steel bridges that give dramatic views of the craggy cliffs below. Of note is the Sanctuary of Madonna della Scala, cut into the rock and accessed by a series of steep steps.

The town is also known for its wine and oil production, and the charming **Museo dell'Olio e dell Vino** within the castle walls re-creates the long traditions of both with models, dioramas, carboys, old wine labels and ancient presses, although descriptions are in Italian only. The castle itself, quadrilateral in shape, was built in the Middle Ages on top of a former Roman site, and was reconstructed during the 18th century.

Museo dell'Olio e dell Vino: Open: 9am–1pm & 3.30–6.30pm. Free admission.

Mottola

The most striking aspect of Mottola is the drive towards the town, when the patchwork fields, rolling meadows and drystone walls, reminiscent more of Normandy than southern Italy, suddenly give way to the sight of this hilltop town. Within the town itself are several medieval churches and a labyrinth of whitewashed alleyways.

Palagianello

A sleepy little town that is worth a detour to see the mastery of houses and the Chiesa di San Pietro carved into the limestone quarries, as well as the views across the striking landscape that bring to mind the adventures of Indiana Jones.

Bridge over the ravine at Massafra

Getting away from it all

A visit to the region of Puglia as a whole, as opposed to, say, a city break in Lecce, constitutes 'getting away from it all'. With its still small tourist infrastructure, there is very little here that would compare with holidays in the nearby Mediterranean or Aegean. Most visitors venturing only minutes off the beaten track will find themselves at the heart of a traditional southern Italian lifestyle, unchanged for decades and somewhat bemused by foreign presence.

However, there are specific aspects of the region and beyond that allow just that extra amount of relaxation, privacy or adventure.

Coastal regions

While it cannot be stressed enough that Puglia is not a destination for a full-on beach holiday, both in terms of natural and commercial facilities, there are coastal areas that make for a pleasant day on the coast. Gallipoli's beaches are some of the best in the region, but travel a few minutes east of the city and you'll find much quieter sandy coves where, out of high season, you may have stretches of sand all to yourself. On the Adriatic coast, the landscape is rocky and craggy in large part, but areas such as Torre dell'Orso

Seaside towns are the best places to find fresh fish

You can always find deserted beaches such as this one in Gallipoli, especially out of season

near Otranto (*see pp90–91*) have small swathes of sandy beach, and the waters are ideal for windsurfing. In addition, all the coastal areas benefit from simple but superb seafood restaurants where the menu is as fresh as that day's catch.

Greece

For a short and enjoyable excursion from Puglia, cross the Adriatic by ferry to the Peloponnese region of Greece. Ferries leave the ports of Bari and Brindisi daily to make the overnight crossing to Patras, itself the third-largest city in Greece and a vibrant port town. From here, it is a drive or bus ride (approximately two hours) to the site of Ancient Olympia, birthplace of the Olympic Games, with a large excavated area of ruined temples and

an excellent museum exploring the history of the ancient sports. An overnight ferry back to Italy, and this two-night break will have added an intriguing dimension to your holiday.
All Greek Ferries:
www.allgreekferries.gr
Superfast Ferries: www.superfast.com

Isole Tremiti

These small islands off the coast of the Gargano Peninsula (*see p34*) do get busy in high season, largely with Italians who have preserved their 'secret' for years. Nevertheless, their small size and sense of hidden wonders still make the islands a great getting-away-from-it-all stopover, particularly if you want a break from a holiday that is otherwise dominated by towns and sightseeing.

Masserie and *trulli* accommodation

For a special and peaceful stay in the Puglian countryside, away from town and city hotels, there are two wonderful options. Many of the area's former *masserie* (farmhouses) have now been restored and converted into guest accommodation, from the simple and rustic to the luxurious. Here, surrounded by olive groves and vineyards, you'll be treated to traditional cuisine, authentic décor and only the call of a sheep or a goat as the background soundtrack. While most are no more than a 15-minute drive or so from major sights in the region, they make a lovely getaway at the end of each day, far from the traffic noise prevalent even in the smallest village.

www.masseriedellapuglia.com

In addition, many of the charming *trulli* of the region have been renovated as tourist accommodation. Spending a few nights in these squat, round buildings is a wonderful way to imagine yourself a peasant farmer

Some *trulli* are available to rent

Spend time in the tranquil Gargano Peninsula

in days gone by – with most of the modern-day facilities thrown in (*see pp64–5*).

Natural beauty

Puglia's only national park is the Umbra Forest in the Gargano Peninsula (*see pp36–7*). This makes for lovely day hikes, cycle routes, and the only opportunity in the region to fully immerse yourself in nature without the soft whirr of agricultural practices in the background. More than 11,000ha (27,180 acres) of pine and chestnut forests are the natural habitat of eagle owls, deer, foxes and hares, as well as more than 50 species of orchid.
www.parcogargano.it (Italian language only); www.gargano.it

Spas

The area around Santa Cesarea Terme in the Salentine Peninsula (*see p96*) has long been known for its thermal waters, and there are spa centres where you can lie back and enjoy therapeutic and relaxing massages, mud baths, steam rooms and more. Many of the upmarket *masserie* (farmhouses) now also include spa treatments and thalassotherapy centres in their programmes, in particular, making much use of the beneficial health qualities of the local olive oil.
Terme di Santa Cesarea.
Via Roma 40. Tel: (0836) 944070.
www.termesantacesarea.it

Practical guide

Puglia is genuinely a year-round destination with warm summers and mild winters. That said, July and August are typically very hot indeed, making anything more than a sunbathing holiday uncomfortable and unpleasant. These are also the months that Italians themselves holiday, and so beaches are likely to be overcrowded and hotel prices at their highest.

When to go

If you're planning to tour the region, the best times for both climate and fewer crowds are spring (April–early June) and early autumn (September–October). The geographical position of Italy's 'heel' also means that it is subject to the two European wind patterns: the *sirocco* in summer and the *maestrale* in winter, although these are unlikely to have any major effect on the average holiday trip. The 'shoulder' months either side of high season, April and October, are still mild and warm, and hotels will be less than full so the tariffs will be good. Rainfall is never significant but is most likely to occur between November and February, and there may be the occasional summer thunderstorm. If, however, you are only visiting Puglia for a beach holiday, be aware that the season here is very short. Most places shut up tight by mid-September and don't reopen again until May, so in the winter months they resemble abandoned ghost towns.

Getting around
By air
Alitalia does operate domestic flights within Italy but the cost of fares is very high, making train travel the most viable option.

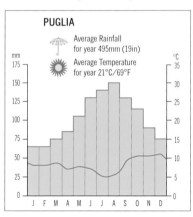

PUGLIA

Average Rainfall for year 495mm (19in)

Average Temperature for year 21°C/69°F

WEATHER CONVERSION CHART

25.4mm = 1 inch

°F = 1.8 × °C + 32

By train

National trains (second-class seating only) cover much of the Puglia region but stop at Lecce. All towns and sights south of Lecce need to be explored by car or bus – there are some local train routes but the timetables are sparse and erratic. Local train tickets need to be bought at the station, either from the ticket office or from ticket machines. Tickets must be validated by stamping them in the machines on the station platform, and the journey must be made within 24 hours of validation. If you forget to stamp the ticket, you will be liable to a fine of around 25 euros by on-board ticket inspectors who are invariably stringent in their duties.
Trenitalia. www.ferroviedellostato.it

By bus

Ferrovie del Sud Est operates both trains and buses within the region, from Bari right down to Santa Maria di Leuca. Tickets can be bought at bus stations.
Bari: Via G Amedola 106/D. Tel: (080) 5462111. Lecce: Viale Oronzo Quarta 38. Tel: (0832) 668111. www.fseonline.it

By car

In order to reach more isolated regions and to minimise journey times between major cities, the easiest way to explore Puglia is by car. All drivers in Italy must carry their current driver's licence with photo ID and, if you're driving your own car, you must carry the vehicle registration document. It is compulsory to wear both front and back seat belts. Cars drive on the right-hand side of the road.

By ferry

Ferry services operate from Bari and Brindisi to Greece (*see p115*), Croatia, Egypt, Turkey and Albania. There are also local ferry services

Hiring a car is the best way to see sights such as the *città bianche*

around the Gargano Peninsula and
to the Isole Tremiti.

Car hire

The major companies of Avis, Budget
and Hertz all have car hire offices in the
major towns. Rates vary according to
rental period and size of car, which
ranges from two-door economy
vehicles through to luxury people
carriers. It is usually possible to hire a
car in one location and drop it off at
the company's offices in another
location.
www.avis.com
www.budget.com
www.hertz.com

Insurance

Third-party insurance is compulsory
and a green card is also recommended.

Not all country roads look like this!

Parking

Most of the main towns and cities in
Puglia have protected the narrow streets
of their old towns by restricting
parking to residents. Visitors need to
park in the specified zones outside
these centres.

Petrol

Petrol (*benzina*) is available in leaded
(*piombo*) and unleaded (*senza piombo*)
form as well as diesel, and petrol
stations in cities and larger towns are
usually open until at least 10pm, while
some are open 24 hours. In smaller,
more rural regions, however, it's
essential to check opening times; many
close as early as 6pm and for the entire
weekend. Currently, petrol prices in
Italy are higher than in Britain,
although diesel is cheaper.

Roads

The standard of roads in Puglia is
generally high. The motorways
(*autostrade*), most of which charge
tolls, are indicated by green signs.
The main motorways into the region
are the A14 from the north and the A16
from the west. Main roads, with blue
signage, are indicated by numbers and
their preceding initials SS, SR or SP
(*strade statali*, *strade regionali* and
strade provinciali).

Security and emergencies

Unfortunately, Puglia has a reputation
for car theft, particularly in areas such
as Bari and Brindisi. Try to park in

Let a boat take the strain for easy sightseeing

busy and populated areas by day and in well-lit areas by night, and always lock your car doors. Don't leave any valuables in your car while it is untended – you're only tempting fate. If you do experience robbery of any kind, report it immediately to the local police. If you're driving in your own car, check with your home automobile club which may have an affiliation with the **Automobile Club d'Italia** (*www.aci.it*). They offer breakdown assistance (*Tel: 116*).

Speed limits

The speed limit in towns and cities is 50kph (30mph), on open roads 90kph (55mph), and on motorways 130kph (80mph). It may not seem like it when you're sharing the road with other Italians, but limits are enforced and speed cameras are in operation on some roads.

RULES OF THE ROAD

In an unofficial sense, and to all intents and purposes, there are no rules of the road. Driving in Puglia, particularly in towns, can be a nerve-racking experience and you'll need your wits about you every second you are behind the wheel. Expect locals to pull out suddenly and without warning, overtake at hairpin bends, turn left or right on red lights if they see an opportunity, keep bumper to bumper in their lane rather than give way to another driver, and blast their horns incessantly if you sit at a green light for a split second. Signage is also erratic – you can find yourself spoon-fed directions for several streets then at a major crossroad or roundabout there will be no indication of which way to go. In towns, signs to hotels and sights are also arbitrary. The best option is to follow the sign to the *centro* (centre), marked by a bull's-eye symbol, find somewhere to park, and locate your destination on foot. In historic centres, narrow streets barely wide enough for a donkey have necessitated one-way systems that, for newcomers, can mean circling the area several times until you find your bearings.

Accommodation

Puglia offers a wide range of accommodation, from traditional hotels and rural farmhouses to self-catering options. Equally, prices vary from the high-end five-star hotels to little more than a few euros per night in family-run affairs. If you're visiting between May and August, it's advisable to book ahead, particularly if visiting the coast. Many northern Italians make the region their annual pilgrimage to sun and sand, and hotels can be block-booked as much as a year in advance.

Hotels

All the main towns and cities have hotels to suit most budgets, and those with a particularly interesting old town, such as Lecce, have many hotels set in converted *palazzi*, which make for an evocative stay. In popular coastal towns such as Gallipoli, Vieste and Otranto, there are typical beach-side hotels that have a rather impersonal air, but they usually have pools and all the facilities you require for a seaside holiday.

It's worth noting that the awarding of hotel stars in the region may not meet with the standards expected elsewhere – a hotel can be awarded four stars simply if it offers a lift and a terrace, for example, while its rooms can be shabby and the staff discourteous. In turn, a rural two- or three-star hotel can be charming and welcoming. If at all possible, ask for recommendations – even the Internet can be misleading, with images shown of elegant squares that may be nowhere near the accommodation in reality.

Agriturismo

Over the past few years, *agriturismo* (rural accommodation) has been a booming business, and many *masserie* (farmhouses) in the countryside have been converted into hotels, occasionally with extremely luxurious facilities. All of them, however, have the unrivalled advantage of being in the heart of nature and offer a very relaxing stay.

Trulli

The most unique accommodation options that Puglia has to offer are the *trulli* (*see pp64–5*) that are dotted around the countryside of the Valle d'Itria. These conical limestone buildings that were once home to farmworkers have now become extremely popular holiday options, either as individual rentals or clustered together to form a hotel complex. Prices are not cheap, particularly in tourist hotspots such as Alberobello, but they do offer an unforgettable experience and the chance to get to the heart of the region.

Camping

There are numerous camping options around Puglia, with sites ranging from the most basic to vast areas with pools, children's facilities, bars and restaurants. Most will charge a small fee if you want to pitch your own tent, as well as offering opportunities to hook up your own caravan, but they also offer bungalows and stationary caravans for rent.
www.camping.it

B&Bs

Italian guesthouses and B&Bs are known as *alberghi* or *pensioni*, and are usually family-run. They offer a cheaper option to hotels, but they will also have fewer facilities – most only offer breakfast and have no evening meal or bar area. While many advertise on the Internet, the tourist offices in the local towns are the best bet to get a full list of what's on offer.

Self-catering

Many of the large *palazzi* in towns such as Lecce have been converted into apartment-style accommodation with basic cooking facilities. This can offer more freedom and a chance to sample produce from local markets. Along the coast, there are numerous apartment complexes usually centred on a shared pool. Inland, many of the farmhouses have now been converted into individual holiday homes, ideal for large families or groups of friends.

A cluster of *trulli* in the countryside near Alberobello

Food and drink

Like all regions of Italy, food is at the heart of Puglia's society and community and is taken very seriously. Locals still tend to shop almost exclusively at markets and in specialised stores rather than following the supermarket trend that has enveloped the rest of Europe.

Meals

Breakfast (*colazione*) usually consists of an espresso or cappuccino coffee, accompanied by a sweet pastry, although most hotels will also offer the savoury options of salami and cheese. Lunch (*pranzo*) is traditionally the main meal of the day and is much lingered over, thanks to the practice of siesta time when shops and businesses close for the majority of the afternoon. There are usually four courses – *antipasto*, which might consist of olives, cold meats and anchovies, not dissimilar to Spanish tapas; *il primo*, which is generally a pasta dish or soup; *il secondo*, the main part of the meal, with a dish of meat or fish (note that vegetables – *contorni* – are ordered separately), and finishing off with *dolce*, which is usually ice cream, cheese or fruit. A coffee rounds off the meal but it *must* be espresso – Italians never end the meal with milky caffeine. Dinner (*cena*) doesn't vary greatly from lunch, although fewer courses may be consumed.

Where to eat

There is a variety of eating establishments in Italy. A *ristorante* is likely to be a fairly grand affair, with tablecloths and uniformed waiters. A *trattoria* is far more informal and usually serves simple meat and pasta dishes. An *osteria* is, literally, a tavern with a limited menu of fresh but simple fare. A *pizzeria* will serve just that – pizza. If you only want a snack, head for a *tavola calda* – literally 'hot table'. Breakfast is often served in bars that pride themselves on their state-of-the-art coffee machines. Note that you'll pay more to have coffee seated at a table than you will standing at the bar. Even the smallest of towns will have a *gelateria* (ice cream parlour) where you can enjoy a choice of flavours.

Puglian specialities

Puglia is a rich agricultural landscape and as such its local produce provides a cuisine that is among the best in Italy. With inland farming and the coast, both meat and fish figure prominently on menus. Vegetarians are not forgotten though, and many restaurants will feature meat-free options.

The abundant wheatfields contribute to the large consumption of pasta, and speciality shapes of the region are *orecchiette* (little ears) and *maccheroncini* (small macaroni), both of which are often added to soups. They are also served in meat sauces or as a vegetarian option, with greens or turnip tops. Lamb is a favourite within the meat category (and sheep's milk is used to create the soft *burrata* cheese), but more delicate diners may be shocked at the frequency with which horse, and even donkey, appear on menus. Mussels, shrimp, oysters and octopus abound on the seafood menus. The more popular vegetables are beans (*fava*), peas (*piselli*) and cabbage (*cavolo*). The enormous *cardoncello* mushrooms are a speciality of the Bari Murgia region and there are numerous festivals in their honour. Chickpeas (*ceci*) are also used in abundance. Among the fruits, figs, melon and grapes are almost always featured.

While you're likely to find pizza anywhere and everywhere, a Puglian speciality is *calzone*, where the dough is folded over around a filling, which usually includes tomatoes, olives, capers, anchovies and cheese, before being baked. Another local speciality that has found its way onto Italian menus around the world is *Parmigiano di melanzane* – aubergine baked with cheese and tomato sauce.

Local bread is often made with black olives, onions, tomato or salami. *Friselle* are hard bread biscuits usually eaten with tomatoes, olive oil and herbs.

Among the sweet delicacies – and Italians are ever fond of their cakes and pastries – are *sospiri* (sighs), small iced sponge cakes filled with cream or jam, and *panetto*, a cake made with figs, raisins, almonds and wine. Local cheeses include *canestrato pugliese*, a hard sheep's milk cheese, and *burrata*, a creamy cheese within a cheese surrounded by a 'skin' of mozzarella.

And, of course, everything is infused with the flavour of top-quality olive oil, the 'liquid gold' that so defines Italian cuisine.

Wine

Despite the fame of Chianti, it is actually Puglia that produces the most wine in Italy, and the industry is taken very seriously indeed. Wine has been produced here since Roman times, and perhaps before, and many of the wines from the region are now DOC (*denominazione d'origine controllata*), meaning they are of the highest quality and have an international reputation. Even those without this official recognition are extremely palatable. Salento is renowned for its red and rosé wines; San Severo, Locorotondo and Ostuni for their whites. When ordering wine in restaurants, it's always worth asking if there is a *vino di casa* (house wine), which can be served in jugs of a *litro* (litre) or *mezzo litro* (half litre).

Food and drink

Puglian wines

Wine has been produced in Puglia since Phoenician times, and Pliny the Elder even mentioned the quality in Roman times. Moreover, despite the fame of 'Chiantishire' in the north, the warm southern climate has ensured that Puglia is the largest wine producer in Italy. In the past, this hasn't always seemed such a good thing – the reputation was for inferior table wine with an eye towards quantity rather than quality. In recent years, however, things have started to change. Many vintners have begun to develop and have made large investments in the techniques of viticulture and in producing far better wines that, nevertheless, have not significantly risen in price. Such moves have attracted the attention of the international wine community, which is now beginning to recognise that some of these wines are of superior quality. Many wine critics have compared the wines produced here to those produced in California, which is hardly surprising as the climate is very similar. This climate means that most Puglian wines have a high level of alcohol, the baking summer sun encouraging a large amount of sugar in the grapes. The highest-quality wines have been awarded with DOC appellation (*denominazione d'origine controllata*), of which there are now 24 produced in Puglia.

The region largely concentrates on red wines, which are perfect accompaniments to red meat and hard cheeses such as pecorino. In Salento, the speciality is the Negro Amaro (literally 'bitter black') grape which produces some of Italy's best reds and rosé wines. The black and white Malvasia grape also produces good wines, and a combination of these two grapes produces the DOC wine Leverano. Other DOC wines of the region include Alezio, Copertino, Galatina, Leverano, Matino, Nardò, Salice Salentino and Squinzano.

The sun makes for sweeter grapes

Puglian vineyard, complete with *trulli*

The area around Castel del Monte is known for its Uva di Troia grape, producing fine reds, while the Canosa di Puglia region combines this grape with Sangiovese to produce Rosso Canosa. Another great red is the very strong Primitivo from the Manduria region. The region's popular rosé is the Aleatico, an excellent accompaniment to light summer *antipasti*. White wine is produced around Gravino and Martina Franca and, of course, in the famous San Severo region.

In total there are 52 red wines, 28 whites, 22 rosés, 17 dessert wines and 9 sparkling wines produced in Puglia today. Possibly the most renowned wine producer in Puglia is Leone de Castris near Lecce, which has won countless international awards.

The grape harvest (*vendemmia*) takes place towards the end of September and into October, and around this time the tourist board of the Puglian wine association (Movimento Turismo del Vino Puglia) organises a variety of tastings and wine tours. For more information, visit *www.mtvpuglia.it*. If you're driving through the country at this time, you'll see local farmers out in the fields picking grapes – an activity that is still very much a family affair – while strapping youths, wearing only swimming trunks, can be seen waist-high in plastic drums treading grapes in the traditional way.

Entertainment

Puglia is not a region to visit if you want high art. Many of the towns will have their own folk music or opera festivals during the summer season, but these are low-key affairs likely to attract only locals. Art museums are also thin on the ground unless you're an aficionado of local artists, although archaeology gets a look-in at almost every town in the region.

All the major towns (Bari, Brindisi, Lecce, Taranto) have at least one if not more cinemas that show both Italian and imported UK and American films, but it should be noted that Italians prefer to dub films (and television programmes) rather than use subtitles, so non-Italian speakers will find cinema trips a challenge. The main city for entertainment of any sophisticated nature is Lecce, where the **Teatro Pubblico Pugliese** (also with a venue in Foggia) presents a variety of plays and performance art (*www.teatropubblicopugliese.it*). There's also a Baroque music festival in the city during September when concerts are performed in a number of churches and other venues in the Old Town. The **Teatro Petruzzelli** in Bari is also a major theatrical venue for the region, particularly for opera. The other main source of entertainment in the region is the year-round calendar chock-full of festivals (*see pp18–19*), when streets come alive to celebrate religious events, harvests and much more.

The Pugliese seem to get their greatest form of entertainment, however, from each other. Every evening, whether it's a big city or a

A bar in Alberobello

A festival bandstand in Conversano

small village, the *passeggiata* is a ritual stroll through the streets, catching up with friends and neighbours after a day's work, and usually meeting up for coffee or ice cream in the innumerable bars and *gelaterie* (ice cream parlours) before indulging in a late dinner, either at home or in a restaurant. Restaurants usually open around 8pm, but they're likely to be fairly deserted for at least an hour after that, with locals preferring to sit down to dinner at around 9.30 or 10pm. For nightlife of a more active kind, discos are usually confined to beach resorts that are only open in summer. Lecce, however, has a number of trendy bars that often stage live music, especially along the Via Federico d'Aragona in the Old Town.

Shopping

Shopping is a delight in Puglia if you like good food. Obviously, one of the main products to take home with you is extra virgin olive oil, produced in the region in abundance and to supreme quality (see pp72–3).

You can find olive oil throughout the region, but the area northwest of Bari, which is covered by the Strada dell'Olio route (*see p57*), is the best bet. Puglian wine (*see pp126–7*) is also of extremely good quality on the whole and at bargain prices compared to those back home. The speciality pasta of the

Alberobello is a good place to pick up souvenirs

region, *orecchiette* (little ears), is sold in souvenir dishes in the more touristy regions, but any town will have a good delicatessen where you can find bags of this and many other shapes, as well as local cheeses and cold meats. In a town that is otherwise something of a tourist trap, one of the most stunning delicatessens can be found: **Maria Concetta Marco** (*via Monte San Michele 37, Alberobello*) is the proprietor of this eponymous gastronomic palace of local specialities, with shelves piled high with jars of artichokes, olives and figs, local pasta, regional wines and a wonderful cheese selection. Maria herself is incredibly friendly and passionate about her stock and is happy to offer tastings.

Lecce is full of quirky little shops in the alleyways of its historic centre, particularly around Via Isabella Castriota, where you can find a number of one-off pieces of art or ornamentation, but the town is also known for its papier mâché. There are

If you buy delicate shells in Gallipoli, wrap them well before packing

numerous shops in the city that sell this craft, but **La Casa dell'Artigianato Leccese** (*Via Matteotti 20, Lecce. Tel: (0832) 306604*) is one of the best. **Il Salotto dell'Arte** (*No 2*) offers a refreshing selection of modern art, verging on Pop Art, which is rarely seen in this part of the country.

Ceramics, particularly from towns such as Grottaglie (*see p111*), make good gifts or souvenirs – just make sure the shopkeeper wraps them securely for travel to avoid breakages.

In terms of clothes and fashion, only the main cities offer any sense of sophisticated style, particularly Lecce, where Via Vittorio Emanuele, leading up to the Duomo, is lined with boutiques, jewellers and leather goods.

Just outside Molfetta, near Bari, is an outlet centre with more than 60 shops, including Stefanel, Calvin Klein and Miss Sixty, selling shoes and clothes at discounted prices.

It should be noted that all shops abide by the local custom of siesta, and close their doors from around 1pm until 5.30pm, which can be frustrating to visitors not used to these hours. However, most also stay open until around 8pm.

Visitors from outside the EU may be able to claim tax back on goods bought from shops in larger cities that display a duty-free sign. You'll need to fill in a form at the time of purchase then present this to customs when departing Italy.

Sport and leisure

Football (calcio) *is not just a sport to most Italians, it's almost a religion. Puglia is no exception, and most towns of any size boast their own stadium. The excitement of match days* (partite) *between the region's big teams such as Lecce (Serie A team), Brindisi and Taranto is palpable in the air, with much flag-flying and tooting of car horns. Tickets are on sale in advance of match days at the clubs themselves, but you'll need photo ID to buy any. For more information, visit* www.footballinitaly.com

In terms of participant sports, however, the region has few designated facilities. The golf course near Bari (*see p149*) is a relatively new feature and the only one

in Puglia of any note. Watersports are largely confined to the areas around Gallipoli, Taranto and Otranto, where windsurfing (and surfing when the

Bikes for hire, Lecce

If you're a golfer, be sure to squeeze in a round while you're in Puglia

waves allow), sea-fishing, diving and snorkelling are options offered by a few local outfits (*see p155*).

Puglia's largely flat landscape does make it an ideal area to explore by bicycle, particularly on the coastal stretch between Bari and Brindisi, and cycling holidays in the region are increasingly in demand with companies such as **Backroads** (*www.backroads.com*), **Hikbik** (*www.hikbik.com*) and **Butterfield and Robinson** (*www.butterfield.com*), the latter including family trips suitable for children. Mountain biking as well as hiking are gradually becoming popular in the rocky landscape of the western Taranto province, but you'll need to bring your own equipment. The variety of the region, from farmland to archaeological sites, lends itself to walking tours, and companies such as **Country Walkers** arrange escorted tours (*www.countrywalkers.com*).

Horse riding is a wonderful way to immerse yourself in the local landscape. Many of the *masserie* (farmhouses) offer horse riding, while **Puglia Imperiale** (*www.pugliaimperiale. com*) offers trips in the Murgia district. For something a little more unusual, the same company also offers hot-air balloon trips.

The main spa area is Santa Cesarea Terme (*see p96*), known for its therapeutic waters, but facilities these days are rather basic and old-fashioned compared to counterparts in the rest of Europe. Many of the *masserie* (*see p122*) also offer spa and other well-being treatments to guests.

Children

Italians love children, and even the smaller towns will often feature a small playground with slides and swings or small carousels. Most restaurants too are happy to have children as their guests, and children will usually be content with a pizza or a plate of spaghetti – the latter conveniently child-sized as Italians eat pasta as a starter. And, while much of the area might be dominated by cathedrals and churches in terms of sightseeing, older children will enjoy the thrill of roaming around castles.

Fasano Zoo-Safari and Fasanolandia

This is the main site in Puglia catering to children's needs. A vast theme park complex features a zoo area that you can drive around safari-style as ostriches, giraffes and many other exotic animals peer in through your (closed) windows. Signs clearly state that windows should remain closed for safety reasons, and feeding the animals is strictly forbidden. Other highlights include the theme ride area, with giant water slides, a roller coaster and a Ferris wheel, a Puglia in miniature that re-creates all the well-known buildings of the region such as Castel del Monte at knee-height. Recent additions to this part of the park include the Eurofighter, a terrifying new, only-for-the-brave roller coaster that promises death-defying loops; plus a dinosaur exhibition and a 4D cinema. The sea life area features penguins and seals and, in 2010, only the third polar bear to be born in situ in Fasano.

Via dello Zoosafari, Fasano. Tel: (080) 4414455. www.zoosafari.it. Open: Dec & Feb Sun 10am–3.30pm, Mar Sat & Sun 9.30am–4pm, Apr–Sept daily 9.30am–4pm (until 5pm Jul & Aug), Oct Wed–Mon 10am–3.30pm, Nov Sat & Sun 10am–3.30pm. Admission charge (rides are extra).

Gondola rides at Zoo-Safari

There's so much to see in the safari park

Essentials

Arriving in Puglia
By air

The introduction of low-cost flights to both Bari and Brindisi has significantly opened up Puglia to international tourism. **Ryanair** (*www.ryanair.com*) operates flights from London Stansted to both airports for as little as £20, but it is essential to book as much in advance as possible. The new flight routes are equally popular with Pugliese who want to travel to the UK, and so seats are at a premium. Ryanair also offers a service between Frankfurt and Bari. Bari airport is 15km (9 miles) from the city centre, with a shuttle bus service into town every 30 minutes; Brindisi airport is 2km (1¼ miles) from its centre. The nearest international airport that serves other areas of Europe and the world is Naples.

By train

Trenitalia is the national rail network and offers various services to Puglia. Eurostar and Intercity are both high-speed trains operating between the country's major cities, and they offer a service from Milan and Bologna to Bari. Seating is offered in both first and second class. Tickets for international or national routes can be purchased via travel agents, online or at station ticket offices.
Trenitalia. www.ferroviedellostato.it

By car

The main motorways (*autostrade*) into the region are the A14 from the north and the A16 from the west.

By sea

Ferries serve the ports of Bari and Brindisi between Puglia and Greece, Croatia, Albania, Turkey and Egypt.

Customs

EU citizens may import and export reasonable amounts of alcohol, tobacco and perfume provided they are over the age of 18 and the amounts are considered to be for personal use and not for resale. For visitors from outside the EU, the restrictions on importing are as follows:

200 cigarettes; or 100 cigarillos; or 50 cigars; or 250g of tobacco

60cc of perfume

4 litres of still table wine

250cc of eau de toilette

1 litre of spirits or strong liqueurs over 22 per cent volume; or 2 litres of fortified wine, sparkling wine or other liqueurs

£390 worth of all other goods including gifts and souvenirs.

Electricity

Italy uses 220 volts and two-pin European plugs. A transformer is required for US appliances.

Bari's harbour is also home to ferries serving neighbouring countries

Internet

Italy has embraced the World Wide Web, and Internet facilities can be found in most towns. Many hotels also offer Internet access.

Money

Italy's currency is the euro (€), and notes are issued in denominations of 5, 10, 20, 50, 100, 200 and 500 euros. Coins are issued in denominations of 1, 2, 5, 10, 20 and 50 cents and 1 and 2 euros.

You can order euro notes ahead of your trip from Thomas Cook, American Express and other exchange services, but there are also ATMs/cashpoint machines at the airports and throughout the cities.

Banks and ATMs

Banks are open from 8.30am to 1.30pm and from 2.30 to 4pm on weekdays, and they close on Saturdays and Sundays. The easiest way to avoid the exchange bureaux is by using your credit or debit card in ATMs/cashpoint machines (*bancomat*). Check with your bank to make sure that your personal identification number (PIN) gives you access to ATMs abroad. ATMs are available at most banks, and accept Visa, Cirrus, Eurocheque and other international cards.

Credit cards

Most of the major credit cards are accepted in all but the smallest of restaurants and shops.

Traveller's cheques

It's always good to have some traveller's cheques to hand when you travel. Try to get them in different denominations, and keep the purchase agreement and a record of the cheques' serial numbers in a different place from the actual cheques.

The most widely accepted traveller's cheques are those from **Thomas Cook** (*www.thomascook.com*) and **American Express** (*www.americanexpress.com*). If the cheques are lost or stolen, be sure to report the theft to the issuing company immediately. In most cases, the cheques will be replaced within 24 hours.

On euro traveller's cheques, you should not have to pay any commission when exchanging them for euros. For other currency cheques, there is usually a commission charge of 1 per cent of the amount changed. Both Thomas Cook and American Express sell euro traveller's cheques.

Opening hours

Shops are usually open 9am–12.30pm and 4–7pm Monday to Saturday.

It's best to call ahead for opening times if you want to visit places such as Lecce's Sedile art gallery

Banks are open 8.30am–1.30pm and 2.30–4pm Monday to Friday, although some in larger cities may open on Saturday mornings. Any visitor to Puglia should be aware of the siesta tradition, which lasts far longer here than in most European regions. In all but the larger towns, everything, including shops and bars, closes from around 1pm and doesn't reopen until around 5pm. This can be extremely frustrating for people used to a more 24-hour lifestyle, and you'll find it difficult even to buy a bottle of water within these hours, so it's best to carry basic provisions with you.

Passports and visas

Citizens of the UK, Ireland, US, Canada, Australia and New Zealand need only a valid passport to enter Italy and do not require visas for stays of up to 90 days. Citizens of South Africa must have visas to enter Italy. Citizens of EU countries may stay without a visa for an unlimited period.

Pharmacies

Farmacie (pharmacies) are identified by a green cross. Italian pharmacists are qualified to give informal medical advice on minor ailments as well as dispensing prescriptions. Make sure you know the generic as well as the brand name of your regular medicines, as they may be sold under a different name in Italy. A list of the nearest late-night pharmacies will be posted on all pharmacy doors after closing time.

Post

Most towns have a post office (*ufficio postale*) with opening hours of 8.30am–1.30pm, Monday to Saturday. Stamps (*francobolli*) can also be bought at tobacconist shops (*tabaccherie*). Italy's postal system can be slow, so mail may take a little longer to reach the destination than it would from other European countries.

Public holidays

The following are national public holidays in Italy, although many local regions have their own holidays during festivals.

1 Jan – New Year's Day

6 Jan – Epiphany

Mar–Apr – Easter weekend

25 Apr – *Anniversario della Liberazione* (Liberation Day)

1 May – *Festa del Lavoro* (Labour Day)

15 Aug – *Ferragosto* (Assumption)

1 Nov – *Ognissanti* (All Saints' Day)

8 Dec – *Immocolata Concezione* (Immaculate Conception)

25 Dec – *Natale* (Christmas Day)

26 Dec – *San Stefano* (St Stephen's Day)

Smoking

Since 2004, smoking has been banned in all indoor public places. This includes restaurants, bars and hotels, although smoking is permitted at outside tables.

Suggested reading

Listings magazines

There are no designated English-language listings magazines in Puglia. The best way to find out what's on during your stay is to visit the local tourist office.

Further reading

Castel Del Monte: Geometric Mystery of the Middle Ages by Heinz Götze (Prestel Verlag, 1998)
Between Salt Water and Holy Water: A History of Southern Italy by Tommaso Astarita (W W Norton & Co Ltd, 2005)
Frederick II: A Medieval Emperor by David Abulafia (Pimlico, 2002)
A Taste of Southern Italy: Delicious Recipes and a Dash of Culture by Marlena De Blasi (Ballantine Books, 2006).

Sustainable tourism

Thomas Cook is a strong advocate of ethical and fairly traded tourism and believes that the travel experience should be as good for the places visited as it is for the people who visit them. That's why we firmly support The Travel Foundation, a charity that develops solutions to help improve and protect holiday destinations, their environment, traditions and culture. To find out what you can do to make a positive difference to the places you travel to and the people who live there, please visit *www.makeholidaysgreener.org.uk*

Tax

Italian IVA (VAT) tax is charged at 20 per cent. Non-EU citizens can claim back tax paid on goods if purchased in shops that display a duty-free shopping sign. You will need to fill in a form at the time of purchase and present this to customs on departure.

Telephones

From within Italy, the dialling code for Bari and the north of Puglia is *080*; for Lecce and the south of Puglia it is *0832* or *0833*.

Calling home from Puglia

Use the following codes, plus the area code (without first 0):
UK: *00 + 44*
Republic of Ireland: *00 + 353*
US and Canada: *00 + 1*
Australia: *00 + 61*
New Zealand: *00 + 64*

Calling Puglia from abroad

To call Puglia from abroad, dial the access code *00* from the UK, Ireland and New Zealand; *011* from the US and Canada; *0011* from Australia, followed by the code for Italy *39*, then the local number including the dialling code.

Mobile phones

In Italy, mobile phones work on the GSM European standard. Before you leave home, make sure you have made the necessary roaming arrangements with your company.

UK, New Zealand and Australian mobile phones will work in Italy, but US and Canadian handsets will not. You can buy universal mobiles from **Mobal Rental** – a UK firm that deals in international communications (*Tel: 1 543 426 999. Fax: 1 543 426 126. US: Tel: 888 888 9162 (free call) or 212 785 5800. www.mobal.com*). Their mobiles work anywhere in the world with a permanent UK number that travels with you.

Time zone

Italy is on Central European Time (GMT + 1 hour).

Toilets

Train and bus stations are the best options for toilets, although don't expect them to be spotless. Museums and galleries also have toilet facilities. Most cafés and restaurants have public facilities for patrons only, so you may have to buy a drink first. In some cases, an attendant doles out *carta* (toilet paper) and expects a small tip in return. In Italy in general, toilets run the gamut from clean and modern to a hole in the floor, so it's advisable to carry packets of sanitary wipes with you at all times.

Travellers with disabilities

In general, Italy is still behind in catering for the disabled, and old buildings and cobbled streets can make getting around challenging. Contact an agency before departure

Essentials

CONVERSION TABLE

FROM	TO	MULTIPLY BY
Inches	Centimetres	2.54
Feet	Metres	0.3048
Yards	Metres	0.9144
Miles	Kilometres	1.6090
Acres	Hectares	0.4047
Gallons	Litres	4.5460
Ounces	Grams	28.35
Pounds	Grams	453.6
Pounds	Kilograms	0.4536
Tons	Tonnes	1.0160

To convert back, for example from centimetres to inches, divide by the number in the third column.

for more details: **Accessible Italy** (*www.accessibleitaly.com*) or **Vacanze Serene** (*Tel: 800 271 027*). **RADAR** (*www.radar.org.uk*) is a UK-based organisation that sells packs for a nominal fee which give detailed advice for travellers with disabilities abroad.

Baroque statue decoration in Lecce

Language

In the larger towns of Bari, Brindisi, Taranto and Lecce, you are likely to find English-speakers, and hotel staff will usually have a good grasp of English. Outside these areas, however, the landscape is almost entirely Italian-speaking so it's a good idea to have a few words for pleasantries and to carry a phrase book for other eventualities.

PRONUNCIATION

c and cc = ch if before e and i, as in cheap

ch = before e and i, is hard, like a k

g and gg = soft, like a j if before e and i

gh = hard, as in go

g = soft, rolling sound with the g almost silent

gn = ny (the g becomes an n sound and the n becomes a y sound)

q = kw, as in quick

sc = soft before an e or an i, as in shed

sch = hard, as in skip

z = ts except when it starts a word, then ds

NUMBERS

1	uno	(oo-noh)
2	due	(doo-eh)
3	tre	(treh)
4	quattro	(kwat-roh)
5	cinque	(chin-kweh)
6	sei	(say)
7	sette	(set-teh)
8	otto	(ott-toh)
9	nove	(noh-veh)
10	dieci	(dee-ay-chee)
20	venti	(ven-tee)
100	cento	(chen-toh)
1000	mille	(mee-leh)

DAYS OF THE WEEK

Monday	lunedì	(loo-ned-dee)
Tuesday	martedì	(mah-ted-dee)
Wednesday	mercoledì	(mehr-col-led-dee)
Thursday	giovedì	(joh-vay-dee)
Friday	venerdì	(ven-neh-dee)
Saturday	sabato	(sab-ah-toh)
Sunday	domenica	(doh-men-ee-cah)

EVERYDAY EXPRESSIONS

Yes	Sì	(*see*)
No	Non	(*noh*)
There is/are	C'è/Ci sono	(*ch-ay/chee son-noh*)
There is/are not	Non c'è/Non ci sono	(*noh ch-ay/noh chee son-noh*)
I want	Voglio	(*voll-ee-oh*)
How much?	Quanto?	(*kwan-toh*)
Expensive	Caro/cara	(*car-oh/car-ah*)
Cheap	A buon mercato	(*ah bwon mayr-cah-toh*)
Money	Soldi	(*sol-dee*)
Toilet	La toilette	(*lah twah-let-teh*)
Men's toilet	Signori	(*seen-yor-ree*)
Women's toilet	Signore/Dame	(*seen-yor-reh*)

GREETINGS AND POLITENESS

Hello	Ciao	(*chow*)
Goodbye	Arriverderci	(*aree-vahr-dahr-chee*)
Good morning	Buon giorno	(*bwon jor-noh*)
Good afternoon	Buona sera	(*bwo-nah say-rah*)
Good evening	Buona sera	(*bwo-nah say-rah*)
Good night	Buona notte	(*bwo-nah not-teh*)
Please	Per favore	(*payr fav-or-ray*)
Thank you	Grazie	(*grah-tzee-ay*)
Excuse me	Scusi/Permesso	(*skoo-see/payr-mess-oh*)
	(to get past someone	

TIME

Today	Oggi	(*oj-jee*)
Yesterday	Ieri	(*ee-eh-ree*)
Tomorrow	Domani	(*doh-mah-nee*)
What is the time?	Che ore sono?	(*keh or-reh sohn-noh*)

Emergencies

Emergency numbers
Police: *112* or *113*
Fire: *115*
Ambulance: *118*

Medical services
Casualty
By law, all hospital accident and emergency rooms must treat all emergency cases for free. If you need urgent medical care, go to the *pronto soccorso* (casualty department). The major hospitals in the region can be found in Foggia, Fasano, Brindisi, Bari and Lecce.

Doctors
EU nationals with a European Health Insurance Card (EHIC) can consult a national health service doctor free of charge, and any drugs prescribed can be bought at chemists at prices set by the Health Ministry. Tests and outpatient treatment are charged at fixed rates. Non-EU nationals who consult a health service doctor will be charged a fee at the doctor's discretion, so make sure you have adequate health insurance.

Opticians
Replacement lenses can usually be fitted overnight, and most opticians will replace a missing screw or make adjustments on the spot. See also *Ottica* (Optics) in the Yellow Pages.

Health and insurance
As of 2006, the European Health Insurance Card (EHIC), valid for five years, replaced the E111 form. The Australian Medicare system also has a reciprocal healthcare agreement. Residents of other countries should ensure that they take out adequate health insurance before leaving home.

Vaccinations are not required, and Italy does not present any serious health worries. The worst that will probably happen to you is suffering from extreme heat in summer or from an upset stomach. Drink bottled water as opposed to tap water, and definitely avoid drinking from fountains. Most minor ailments can be diagnosed and treated at pharmacies (*farmacie*).

Safety and crime
Southern Italy has a justified reputation for petty crime and car theft. In the narrow medieval alleyways of places such as Bari's Old Town, bag-snatching is a real possibility. Keep all your money and valuables out of sight, and preferably wear a money belt under your clothes. Don't leave your car in a dark or secluded place and again keep valuables out of sight. Women should avoid walking alone at night.

Embassies and consulates
There are no foreign embassies in Puglia – the nearest embassies are in

Rome (*see below*). There is, however, a
British Honorary Consul in Bari:
Via Dalmazia 127. Tel: (080) 5543668.

Embassies in Rome
Australia
Via Antonio Bosio. Tel: 06 852 721.
www.italy.embassy.gov.au

Canada
Via Zara 30. Tel: 06 445 981.
www.canadainternational.gc.ca/italy

Ireland
Piazza Campitelli 3. Tel: 06 697 9121.
www.embassyofireland.it

New Zealand
Via Clitunno 44. Tel: 06 853 7501.
www.nzembassy.com

UK
*Via XX Settembre 80a. Tel: 06 422
00001. www.fco.gov.uk*

US
Via Veneto 121. Tel: 06 46 741.
www.usembassy.it

Italian embassies and consulates abroad
Australia
*12 Grey St, Deakin, Canberra, ACT.
Tel: +61 2 6273 3333.
Fax: +61 2 6273 4223.
www.ambcanberra.esteri.it*

Canada
275 Slater St, 21st floor,
*Ottawa ON K1P 5H9.
Tel: +1 613 232 2401.
Fax: +1 613 233 1484.
www.ambottawa.esteri.it*

Ireland
*63–65 Northumberland Rd, Dublin.
Tel: +353 1 660 1744.
Fax: +353 1 668 2759.
info@italianembassy.ie*

New Zealand
*34–38 Grant Rd, Box 463,
Thorndon, Wellington.
Tel: +64 4 473 5339.
www.ambwellington.esteri.it*

UK
*14 Three Kings Yard, Davies St,
London W1Y 2EH.
Tel: +44 20 7312 2200.
Fax: +44 20 7312 2230.
www.amblondra.esteri.it*

US
*3000 Whitehaven St, NW,
Washington, DC 20008.
Tel: +1 202 612 4400.
Fax: +1 202 518 2154.
www.ambwashingtondc.esteri.it*

Police
Every village and town has a police
station (*carabinieri*) where you must go
to report any crime. The police will give
you a document confirming that you
have made the report, and you will
need this to claim anything back on
your travel insurance.

Directory

Accommodation price guide

Prices are per double room, per night.
Breakfast included unless otherwise stated.

★	up to €75
★★	€75–125
★★★	€125–250
★★★★	over €250

Eating out price guide

Prices are for an average three-course
meal for one, excluding drinks.

★	up to €15
★★	€15–30
★★★	€30–45
★★★★	over €45

FOGGIA

Foggia

ACCOMMODATION

Mercure Cicolella ★★★
This luxury chain hotel
has a central location
and is housed in a
converted *palazzo*,
with spacious and
comfortable rooms.
There's also an acclaimed
restaurant that has the
added benefit of terrace
seating in summer.
*Viale 24 Maggio 60.
Tel: (0881) 566111.*

EATING OUT

**Osteria dello Zio
Aldo ★★★**
'Uncle Aldo' of the
restaurant's name still
presides over this local
favourite, which prides
itself on the freshest of
local produces. The
seafood pastas, with
clams or squid, are
superb, there's a good
wine list and the choice
of cheeses is excellent.
*Via Arpi 61. Tel: (0881)
708104.*

Ventaglio ★★★
Probably the best
restaurant in town. Set in
a 19th-century building,
with outside seating, the
menu combines the best
of local produce with
innovative cooking
techniques. Try the salted
cod (*baccalà*) with sugar
and olives.
*Via G Postiglione 6.
Tel: (0881) 661500.
Closed: Mon (& weekends
Jul & Aug).*

ENTERTAINMENT

Teatro Giordano
Named after the town's
native composer
Umberto Giordano, this
is the area's only real
theatrical venue, staging
plays, opera and
concerts.
*Piazza Cesare Battisti 21.
Tel: (0881) 774640.*

Isole Tremiti

ACCOMMODATION

Gabbiano ★★★
Wonderful views and
comfortable rooms. A
shuttle service runs to
and from the port.
*Piazza Belvedere, San
Domino. Tel: (0882)
463410.*

Manfredonia

ACCOMMODATION

Panorama del Golfo ★★
Just 3km (2 miles)
outside town, this
small hotel (32 rooms)
is housed in a
17th-century building
right on the waterfront.

All rooms have a balcony, and the on-site restaurant is known for its local cuisine.
Lungomare del Sole 34, Siponto. Tel: (0884) 542843. www. hotelpanoramadelgolfo.it
Regiohotel Manfredi
★★★
Just outside town, this is a lovely family-oriented place to stay, with a small children's playground and a pool with a water slide. For adults, it offers an elegant and comfortable stay, with all the mod cons and a friendly atmosphere.
SP58, 12km (8 miles) from Manfredonia. Tel: (0884) 530122. www.regiohotel.it

Peschici
ACCOMMODATION
Elisa ★★
This restored 16th-century building offers 31 renovated rooms with modern comforts and a lovely position near the beach. The restaurant serves food that is typical of the Gargano region and accommodation is half board.
Via Marina 20.

Tel: (0884) 964012. www.hotelelisa.it. Open: Apr–Sept.

San Giovanni Rotondo
ACCOMMODATION
Gran Paradiso ★★
Not far from the church dedicated to Padre Pio (*see p29*), this is a modern but smart hotel with a relaxing and romantic atmosphere. The large restaurant is also one of the town's best.
Viale A Moro 125. Tel: (0882) 454894.
D'Amato ★★★
Only a few steps from the beach, this 4-star hotel is the best in this small town, with a lovely Mediterranean feel and personal service from the owners themselves.
Località Spiaggia. Tel: (0884) 963415. www.hoteldamato.it. Open: Apr–Sept.

EATING OUT
Osteria Antica Piazzetta ★★
In the heart of the Old Town, the food here is simple but delicious – home-made pasta, fish of the day, mixed meat grill, local cheeses and more.

Via Al Mercato 13. Tel: (0882) 451920. Closed: Wed and Jan & Jul.
L'Antico Mugnale ★★★
Set in a former church in the heart of the Old Town, the menu here focuses entirely on fish – the 'catch of the day', either baked or grilled, is invariably the best option, but the seafood pastas are always good too.
Via San Lorenzo 79. Tel: (0884) 538415. Closed: Sun night, Mon & for 2 weeks in Jul.

Vieste
ACCOMMODATION
Hotel Magnolia ★
A little out of the town centre but refreshingly away from the main drag of faceless hotels, the Magnolia has a lovely pool with hot tub, friendly and helpful staff and spotless en-suite rooms.
Via Macchia di Mauro 8. Tel: (0884) 708838. www. magnoliahotelvieste.com
Hotel Punta San Francesco ★
Clinging on to the cliffside, there is a lovely sunbathing area here with striking sea views.

Rooms are basic but clean, and there's a communal bar area.
Via San Francesco 2.
Tel: (0884) 701422. www.
hotelpuntasanfrancesco.it

Hotel Seggio ★★
Set in a 17th-century building in the historic centre of town with sea views and a lovely swimming pool.
Via Veste 7.
Tel: (0884) 708123.
www.hotelseggio.it

Villa Candida ★★★
Two kilometres (1¼ miles) from the main town, this lovely complex, set around an elegant pool, is surrounded by olive and pine trees. There are 15 apartments with kitchen facilities.
Località Defensola.
Tel: (0884) 701852. www.
residencevillacandida.it

EATING OUT

Box 19 ★
A wonderful fresh fish counter greets you as you enter this friendly restaurant, which is decorated in traditional style with stone alcoves. The menu lives up to the display, with seafood antipasti such as grilled squid, a variety of fish and *spaghetti vongole* served in a deep shell.
Via S Maria di Merino 13. Tel: (0884) 705229.

SPORT AND LEISURE

Associazione Gargano Bike
This company offers half-day bike tours of the Gargano National Park, with varying themes, such as visits to olive oil factories and historic farmhouses.
Località Defensola.
Tel: (0884) 704186.

ExploraGargano
Another outfit that offers half-day tours of the Gargano Peninsula on mountain bikes, between Vieste and Peschici, visiting both natural and archaeological sites.
Via V Valeri 13.
Tel: (0884) 708976.

BARI
Alberobello
ACCOMMODATION
I Trulli dell'Aia Antica ★★
Five minutes outside town, this B&B has the wonderfully unusual setting of a traditional *trullo* yet with modern and comfortable facilities.
Via Capitolo, Zona B.
Tel: (080) 4383088.
www.trulliaiaantica.it

Trulli Holiday
A company that offers *trulli* accommodation around the region, in beautifully romantic style. Prices vary from reasonable to luxury, depending on season.
Piazza A Curri 1.
Tel: (080) 4325970.
www.trulliholiday.com

Andria
ACCOMMODATION
La Grandetta ★
Just a stone's-throw from the impressive Castel del Monte (*see pp49–51*) and set sympathetically within the wilderness of the Murgia region, this is a wonderfully peaceful B&B that also benefits from a lovely veranda and barbecue area. There are only three rooms so it's vital to book in advance.
Località Castel del Monte, SP 234.
Tel: (0883) 599517.
www.lagrandetta.it

Bari

ACCOMMODATION

Villa del Mar ★★

Recently renovated, this is a charming seafront B&B. All rooms are en-suite with flatscreen TVs and Internet access and all also benefit from a balcony. Parking is also free which is always a benefit in this traffic-heavy city.

Via Napoli 378.
Tel: (340) 7535519.
www.villadelmar.it

Palace Hotel ★★★

A grand stalwart of Bari, near the castle, with elegant rooms and antique furniture. Also caters well for business travellers.

Via Lombardi 13.
Tel: (080) 5216551.
www.palacehotelbari.it

EATING OUT

Pignata ★★★★

The best place in town for traditional but elegant Puglian cuisine – try the beans with chicory – and an excellent wine list of local vintages.

Corso Vittorio Emanuele 173. Tel: (080) 5232481.
Closed: Mon & Aug.

Varvamingo ★★★★

A lovely *osteria* not far from the harbour. Both indoor and outdoor dining with beautifully laid tables dressed in crisp white cotton. There's a heavy influence of seafood here served with pasta. Fresh fish and seafood served by the kilo. The wine list is extensive to say the least.

Via Garibaldi 4. Tel: (080) 5433658.

ENTERTAINMENT

Matisse Café Concert

In the Old Town, just off Piazza Mercantile, this small bar features a regular programme of live music and local DJs.

Piazza Ferrarese 10.

Teatro Kismet Opera

A long and varied range of theatrical entertainment, from the avant-garde to Shakespeare, all in Italian.

Strada San Giorgio Martire 22/F. Tel: (080) 5797667.
www.teatrokismet.org

Teatro Piccinni

Named after a local playwright, this is one of Bari's main theatrical venues.

Corso Vittorio Emanuele 1. Tel: (080) 5212484.

SPORT AND LEISURE

Barialto Golf Club

Just 20 minutes' drive south of Bari, golf lovers can practise their swing at this 18-hole course, surrounded by palm and olive trees. A day's play costs around €50 per person.

Cassamassina, SS100.
Tel: (080) 6977105.

Bisceglie

ACCOMMODATION

Hotel Salsello ★★

A slightly dated 1970s-style hotel with adjacent bar and restaurant. The rooms are spacious and nicely fitted out, some with balconies overlooking the sea, and there's a pool.

Via Vito Siciliani 42.
Tel: (080) 3955953.
www.hotelsalsello.com

I Cigni ★★

Simple but comfortable hotel accommodation in the centre of the Old Town.

Via G Bovio 258.
Tel: (080) 3955761.

Nicotel ★★★

The smartest hotel in town on a street leading

down to the sea. Elegant public and private rooms and a good restaurant. *Via della Libertà.* *Tel: (080) 3993111.*

Conversano

EATING OUT

Pashà ★★★

Overlooking the castle, this lovely intimate restaurant is further enhanced by its friendly, family-run atmosphere. The food is based on local traditions – try the roasted goat with potatoes. *Piazza Castello 5–7.* *Tel: (080) 4951079.* *Closed: Tue.*

Monopoli

ACCOMMODATION

Masseria Curatori ★

Very much a working farm, the rooms here are simple but charming. There's one self-contained apartment too. Breakfast is served with the family owners. *Contrada Cristo delle Zolle 227, Monopoli.* *Tel: (080) 777472.*

Trani

ACCOMMODATION

Riviera ★

On the seafront, this 16th-century building has been converted into a modern and modest hotel with a friendly atmosphere. *Via Galilei 6.* *Tel: (088) 3403222.* *www.hotelrivieratrani.it*

Regia ★★★

This small hotel, facing the cathedral, has carefully converted a 17th-century building into a modern yet evocative place to stay, with original stone walls and polished floors. *Piazza Mons Addazi 2.* *Tel: (088) 3584444.* *www.hotelregia.it*

EATING OUT

Osteria Corteinfiore ★★★

Within a 15th-century *palazzo*, Mediterranean fare is the order of the day here, such as red mullet marinated in sweet vinegar, and pasta with clams. The amaretto parfait offered for dessert should satisfy any sweet tooth. *Via Ognissanti 18.* *Tel: (088) 3508402.* *Closed: Sun evening & Mon.*

BRINDISI

Brindisi

ACCOMMODATION

Mercure GA Internazionale ★★

On the waterfront in an 18th-century building, this elegant hotel has long attracted the rich and famous. As well as standard but stylish rooms, there are ten suites available. Parking on-site. *Lungomare Regina Margherita 23.* *Tel: (0831) 523473.*

EATING OUT

Giubilo ★★

A lovely family-run *trattoria*, serving excellent pizza, right in the city centre. *Via Cavour 36.* *Tel: (0831) 529688.*

Menhir ★★★

The name may recall ancient history in the area, but the restaurant is pure modernity. Specialities are, understandably, seafood – squid, red mullet and tuna carpaccio are among the recommendations. *Via Pacuvio 18.* *Tel: (0831) 568234.*

ENTERTAINMENT

Nuovo Teatro Verdi

The main venue in
the city for concerts,
dance performances
and opera.
Via Santi.
Tel: (0831) 523950.

SPORT AND LEISURE

Aquademia Dive Centre

This centre offers sailing
and diving courses and
excursions.
Via Osanna 63.
Tel: (0831) 525650.
www.aquademiaweb.it

Fasano

ACCOMMODATION

Masseria Narducci ★

A white limestone
farmhouse with a
family-run atmosphere,
adorned with brightly
coloured geraniums.
Lovely vaulted lounge
area and renowned
restaurant. The rooms
are housed in the
converted stable area.
Via Lecce 144, SS16.
Tel: (080) 4810185. www.
agriturismonarducci.it

Masseria Marzalossa ★★

All rooms have their
own courtyard in this
lovely 18th-century
farmhouse. Swimming
pool and lovely
gardens too.
Contrada da Pezze Vicine
65, Fasano.
Tel: (080) 4413024.
www.marzalossa.com

Montalbano

ACCOMMODATION

Massiera Lamiola Piccola ★★

A 17th-century
farmhouse deep in the
countryside yet only
10km (6 miles) from
Ostuni. The simple
rooms are charmingly
furnished with wrought-
iron beds, the lounge
boasts an enormous
original fireplace, and
the on-site restaurant
specialises in
local cuisine.
Contrada da Lamiola
Piccola. Tel: (0831) 359972.
www.lamiolapiccola.com

Relais Masseria Montalbano ★★★

A beautifully renovated
traditional farmhouse in
the countryside not far
from Ostuni, where the
entire 16th-century
village has been
preserved as a tourist
enclave. A stunning
outdoor restaurant
surrounded by a
landscape of olive groves
makes this ideal for a
romantic stay.
SS16. Tel: (0831) 359945.
www.
masseriamontalbano.it

Oria

ACCOMMODATION

Borgo di Oria ★/★★

This company offers a
range of simple yet
comfortable apartments
to rent in this historic
town, which makes for a
good self-catering option.
Tel: (329) 7145093.
www.borgodioria.it

EATING OUT

Alle Corte di Hyria ★

The medieval
atmosphere of the
town is re-created in this
vaulted restaurant
serving standard Italian
fare. Good for children.
Via F Milizia 146.
Tel: (329) 6624507.

Bar Kenia ★

Wonderful home-made
traditional ice cream
in an array of
mouthwatering flavours.
Piazza Manfredi 11.

La Taverna degli Schiavoni ★

Simple but friendly
pizzeria decorated with

bench seating and cushions.
Via Latiano 101.
Tel. (0831) 849552.

Ostuni

ACCOMMODATION

Nonna Isa ★

A small and simple yet welcoming B&B, with communal areas featuring a grand piano and stylish rooms.
Via Vittorio Alfieri 9.
Tel: (0831) 332515.

Il Frantoio ★★

Eight rooms in a converted farmhouse, with a games room, library and grounds that offer orchards and horse riding.
SS16, just outside Ostuni.
Tel: (0831) 330276.
www.masseriailfrantoio.it

Masseria Santa Lucia ★★★

A lovely 4-star resort hotel at Ostuni's marina. There are plenty of sporting options including tennis and golf, and the hotel received an Ecolabel award for sustainable tourism.
SS379, Costa Merlata exit.
Tel: (0831) 3560.
www.masseriasantalucia.it

La Terra ★★★

This 4-star hotel in the centre of the lovely hill town of Ostuni is set in a converted 18th-century *palazzo*, and, while the rooms are stylishly modern, the original stonework has been left exposed to preserve the historic atmosphere.
Via G Petrarolo.
Tel: (0831) 336651.
www.laterrahotel.it

EATING OUT

Osteria del Tempo Perso ★★★

The slightly bizarre décor here of saintly figures in glass cases shouldn't put you off the wonderful local cuisine and friendly service. The antipasti menu (minimum two people) resembles a Greek meze affair with dish upon dish of local specialities emerging from the kitchen, such as cauliflower in herb batter, and buffalo cheese with cured ham. For the main course, the grilled lamb is superb; the donkey meat (*asina*) and horse meat may not appeal to all.

Via Tanzarella Vitale 47.
Tel: (0831) 304819.

Ristorante Porta Nova ★★★

The menu at this homely place concentrates on the very best of the Adriatic, including mussel and clam soup, 'white' grilled prawns and squid. If you're in the mood for meat, the lamb is divine, while the enormous wine list has a superb collection of Puglian offerings.
Via G Petrarolo 28.
Tel: (0831) 338983.

ENTERTAINMENT

Cadillac Café

A popular wine bar that also transforms itself into a disco in the early hours.
Via dei Colli.

Café Parisi

A long list of cocktails, an interior that resembles a Parisian boudoir, and pleasant outside tables in the heart of the Old Town make this a great spot for an early-evening aperitif or post-dinner brandy.
Via Cattedrale.

Gelateria Borgo Antico

In the shadow of the cathedral with a few

outside tables, delicious creamy ice cream is served in a range of cone sizes and a wide range of flavours. Sorbets too.
Piazzetta Cattedrale.

Jimmiz
Outside the main town on the coast, this disco pub offers outdoor dancing in summer and a lively yet stylish atmosphere all year round.
SS379, Gorgognolo Marina di Ostuni.

Madrif
By day a relaxing café, by night a more lively 'American bar' with disco.
Via Cattedrale.

Aqua In
On the coast just outside Ostuni is this water park full of slides, shoots and wave machines.
Torre Pozzella.
Tel: (0831) 968496.

LECCE AND THE SALENTINE PENINSULA
Gallipoli
ACCOMMODATION
La Riviera ★★
A small but beautifully presented B&B right on the waterfront, with walls decorated with murals and frescoes, rooms nicely furnished with traditional pieces, and great views.
Riviera Nazario Sauro.
Tel: (0833) 261096.

Victoria Palace Hotel ★★
A little way out of the main centre, along the Lungomare, but a peaceful and stylish option, with attractive pool area, and efficient, English-speaking staff. Most rooms have balconies and are brightly decorated and include TV and DVD players. There is a shuttle bus to the town in summer.
Via Petrarca.
Tel: (0833) 293040.
www. hotelvictoriagallipoli.it

EATING OUT
Il Capriccio ★★
One of the town's best fish restaurants in a place where you are spoilt for choice for seafood offerings. The spaghetti with sea urchins is a speciality, and the seafood risotto is superb. Elegant interior with vaulted roof.
Viale Bovio 14.
Tel: (0833) 261545.

La Paranza ★★★
Virtually set within the fish market itself, with a lovely sunny terrace and trendy interior. Unsurprisingly offers the freshest catch from the sea possible. The *frutti di mare* platter of oysters, mussels, clams and scallops is a must for seafood lovers.
Largo Dogana.
Tel: (0833) 262400.

ENTERTAINMENT
DOC
A friendly wine bar (and restaurant) also serves as an *enoteca* (wine shop) where the chatty owner will happily guide you through a range of good local wines.
Via Quartini 3.

Teatro Italia
The town's main cinema complex featuring the latest Hollywood releases, although most are dubbed into Italian.
Corso Roma 217.

Lecce

ACCOMMODATION

Azzuretta ★

Apartment-style accommodation within an old *palazzo*, with basic kitchen facilities and a mezzanine-level bedroom. Basic breakfast supplies are brought to you each morning. Monumental staircase.
Via A Vignes 2. Tel: (832) 242211. www.bblecce.it

Casa Elisabetta ★★

The best deal in town in terms of location, cost and quality of service. Set in a striking converted *palazzo* in the heart of the Old Town and the restaurant and bar district, the rooms are simple but smart. There's a lovely outside courtyard beneath the magnificent entrance, as well as a roof terrace. Book ahead.
Via Vignes 15.
Tel: (0832) 307052.
www.beb-lecce.com

Patria Palace Hotel ★★★★

Certainly the best hotel in town and probably the finest in Puglia. Rooms are decorated in traditional but homely style and those at the front have a stunning view of the façade of the Basilica di Santa Croce (*see pp84–5*). There's also a lovely rooftop pergola with views out across the town. The restaurant is renowned for its regional cuisine.
Piazzetta Riccardi.
Tel: (0832) 245111.
www.
patriapalacehotellecce.com

EATING OUT

I Latini ★

Good-value, traditional cuisine in the heart of the historic centre. There are outside tables.
Via Palmieri 46. Tel: (0832) 244111.

Alle Due Corti ★★

An unpretentious *trattoria* in the heart of the historic centre. Menu highlights include the local *orrecchiete* pasta served with turnip tops and a platter of mixed roasted meat, but the menu changes weekly according to seasonal ingredients. The interior features a 15th-century fireplace and the walls are decorated with traditional papier mâché.
Corte dei Giugni 1.
Tel: (0832) 242223.

La Torre di Merlino ★★

A lovely courtyard surrounded by vines and hedges outside, or an interior of banquette-style seating. Lengthy menu of local cuisine, including horse meat, which is a common dish in Puglia. Great pasta and seafood too.
Vico Giambattista del Tufo, off Via Federico d'Aragona.
Tel: (0832) 242091.
www.torredimerlino.it

Blu Notte ★★★

Right on the corner of the Porta San Biagio, this elegant restaurant is known for its fresh fish counter from which you can choose your dinner. The oysters, caught by deep-sea divers near Gallipoli, are superb, and the staff is wonderfully attentive and helpful. There are outside tables.
Via Brancaccio 2.
Tel: (0832) 304286.

ENTERTAINMENT

Allonsanfan

Via Federico d'Aragona is a bustling street in the

centro storico that comes alive with bars and restaurants spilling out on the narrow alleyway at night. Allonsanfan is one of the most popular, particularly with students of the town's university. As well as cocktails and other drinks, Allonsanfan also serves pizza and crêpes.
Via Federico d'Aragona 17.

Greenland Glamour
An achingly trendy wine bar that also shows a full programme of Sky Sports.
Via Taranto 88.

J&H (Dr Jekyll & Mr Hyde)
Just outside Lecce, this popular bar features a disco on Saturday nights, karaoke on Sundays and salsa dancing on Wednesdays.
Via Leuca, 3km (2 miles) from the city centre.

La Negra Tomasa
Lecce loves its 'pubs' (there's an Irish bar and two Scottish pubs in town), and this is one of the best in a street that swarms with watering holes.
Via F d'Aragona 2.

Misvago
A tiny bar/café with a trendy interior decorated with banquettes and psychedelic art. Outside tables look out directly onto the Anfiteatro ruins and the façade of the Chiesa di Santa Maria della Grazia.
Piazza S. Oronzo 22.

Multisala Massimo
This multi-screen cinema complex shows both European and Hollywood films (dubbed into Italian).
Viale Lo Re 3.

Urban Café
Popular bar decorated with red leather and chrome. Loud music and cocktails are the order of the day.
Piazza Vittorio Emanuele.

SPORT AND LEISURE

Marea Diving
Diving courses, snorkelling trips and more are on offer here.
Via Fontanella 37, Santa Cesarea Terme.
Tel: (0836) 811843.
www.mareadiving.it

Orca Diving Centre
Another outlet offering diving courses and excursions around the Salento Peninsula.
Porto Cesareo.
Tel: (349) 5701717.
www.orcadivingcenter.it

Porto Turistico
Yachts and smaller craft can be hired from this marina for boat trips around the area.
Marina di Leuca, Santa Maria di Leuca.
Tel: (0833) 758687.

Smaré Crew
Trips in glass-bottomed boats can be arranged here. You can rent your own canoe or motorboat if you prefer to do things independently. Fishing and scuba diving trips can also be organised.
Via Doppia Croce, Santa Maria di Leuca.
Tel: (0833) 758110.

SpeleoTrekkingSalento
Organised trips to caves and grottoes can be arranged with this company throughout the Salento region.
Tel: (0832) 305678.

Splash!
Just outside Gallipoli, this small water park feature slides and shoots – great fun for kids.
Rivabella.
Tel: (0833) 273400.

www.splashparco.it.
Closed: Oct–May.

Otranto
ACCOMMODATION
Le Dune ★
Not far from the seafront, this basic but comfortable B&B has three en-suite rooms, each with a balcony. Good value and friendly.
Via A Sforza 4.
Tel: (0836) 801130.
www.leduneonline.it
Balconcino d'Oriente ★★
In the heart of the *centro storico*, with views of the castle from the terrace, this is a lovely and evocative B&B with various period as well as oriental details. Rooms are fairly sparse but comfortable.
Via San Francesco da Paola 71. Tel: (0836) 801529.
Torre Pinta ★★
In a valley just outside town, this restored farmhouse offers tranquil accommodation with four-poster beds in converted medieval apartments.
Via delle Memorie.
Tel: (0836) 1902453.
www.torrepinta.it

EATING OUT
Zia Fernanda ★★
On the fringes of the Old Town, seafood is the mainstay of the menu here, including an excellent and hearty fish soup. Booking advisable.
Via XXV Aprile. Tel: (0836) 801884. Closed: Feb.
Peccato di Vino ★★★★
Retaining original stone walls and a traditional fireplace, the emphasis here is on fish, and the very freshest fish at that. The bread is all home-made and the wine list is further enhanced by the experience of the staff.
Via Rondachi 7–9.
Tel: (0836) 801488.

TARANTO
Manduria
EATING OUT
Osteria dei Mercantini ★★
A good place to sample regional cuisine, and there's a large selection of pizzas too.
Via Sen G Lacaita 7.
Tel: (099) 9713673.

Martina Franca
ACCOMMODATION
Giardino degli Aranci ★
Its name means 'garden of oranges' and, at just 1km (²/₃ mile) outside the centre of Martina Franca, this is a delightful place to stay while exploring this Baroque town. Children are particularly welcome.
Via Taranto, SS 172.
Tel: (080) 4856066. www.giardinodegliaranci.biz
Sotto Il Monte ★
Slightly unusual apartment accommodation, with kitchen facilities, living room and bedroom all in one space, separated by screens. However, it's about as central as you can get in the Old Town, and if you're on a tight budget it's a good option.
Vico I Cirillo 5.
Tel: (080) 4805878.
Park Hotel San Michele ★★
This hotel is beautifully situated within its own parkland, complete with pool and small children's play area, all centrally located. The terrace bar and restaurant is a wonderful addition, accompanied by the splash of fountains.
Viale Carella 9.
Tel: (080) 4807053. www.parkhotelsanmichele.it

EATING OUT

Al Dolce Morso ★

A simple but friendly *pizzeria* in the *centro storico*, with outside seating.
Via Giannone 3.
Tel: (080) 4801315.

Cantina del Toscana ★

Under the famous porticoes in the old town, this restaurant serves traditional cuisine such as anchovy antipasto, carpaccio of beef and good pasta dishes like *spaghetti al vongole* (with clams).
Piazza Immacolata.
Tel: (080) 4302827.

Ristorante Ai Portici ★

Next door to the Toscana (above), with a similar if slightly longer menu. The puréed beans are among the more local dishes offered.
Piazza Immacolata.
Tel: (080) 4801702.

Vecchia Lanzo ★★

Just 6km (4 miles) outside town, enjoy traditional Puglian food in the evocative setting of an original *trullo*.
San Paolo Via Taranto.
Tel: (080) 4490733.

ENTERTAINMENT

Caffè Tripoli

A popular *gelateria* and bar in a historic building just seconds from the Basilica di San Martino. A great place to watch the evening *passeggiata* go by.
Via Garibaldi 25.

Gran Caffè

Set on the town's main square (*see pp108–9*), this is an elegant option for a pre- or after-dinner drink, or simply a coffee and ice cream, with tables set beneath cream awnings allowing you to watch the world go by.
Piazza XX Settembre.

Pub Kelly

The obligatory Irish bar that shows sports events and serves basic food, but with a lively atmosphere.
Viale de Gasperi 52.

Taranto

ACCOMMODATION

Ara Solis ★★

Part of the Best Western chain, this modern hotel may look charmless and impersonal on the outside, but its interior provides all the usual comforts, and it also has a pool, a beach, conference facilities and car parking.
Via Calata Penna Dritta 2. Tel: (099) 4710809.

Europa ★★★

A lovely boutique-style hotel overlooking the sea and the Old Town. All the rooms are individually decorated in tasteful style.
Via Roma 2.
Tel: (099) 4525994.
www.hoteleuropaonline.it

EATING OUT

Trattoria Gatto Rosso ★★

An excellent seafood restaurant right in the city centre. Simply prepared (grilled or baked) fish accompanied by seasonal vegetables.
Via Cavour 2.
Tel: (099) 4529875.
Closed: Mon.

SPORT AND LEISURE

Motonave Cala Junco

Departing from the port of the Old Town, cruises around the Gulf of Taranto take in all the main sights from the water.
Tel: (099) 4752859.
www.navecalajunco.it

Index

Acknowledgements

Thomas Cook Publishing wishes to thank ROBIN GAULDIE, to whom the copyright belongs, for the photographs in this book except for the following images:

ALAMY 1, 14, 69, 123
DREAMSTIME 17, 76, 141 (Valeria Cantone), 22 (Faberphoto), 82 (Ivan Paiano), 109 (Milla74)
SARGASSO MEDIA 90, 103
WIKIMEDIA COMMONS 33 (Maartin18), 93 (Colossus), 94 (Freddyballo)
WORLD PICTURES/PHOTOSHOT 35, 110

For CAMBRIDGE PUBLISHING MANAGEMENT LTD:
Project editor: Thomas Willsher
Typesetter: Trevor Double
Proofreaders: Michele Greenbank & Jan McCann
Indexer: Karolin Thomas

SEND YOUR THOUGHTS TO
BOOKS@THOMASCOOK.COM

We're committed to providing the very best up-to-date information in our travel guides and constantly strive to make them as useful as they can be. You can help us to improve future editions by letting us have your feedback. If you've made a wonderful discovery on your travels that we don't already feature, if you'd like to inform us about recent changes to anything that we do include, or if you simply want to let us know your thoughts about this guidebook and how we can make it even better – we'd love to hear from you.

Send us ideas, discoveries and recommendations today and then look out for your valuable input in the next edition of this title.

Emails to the above address, or letters to the traveller guides Series Editor, Thomas Cook Publishing, PO Box 227, Coningsby Road, Peterborough PE3 8SB, UK.

Please don't forget to let us know which title your feedback refers to!